AUSTIN
THE CITY AT A GLANCE

Royal-Texas Memorial Stadium
The university's mammoth American stadium seats more than 100,000, ninth largest arena in the world, bu second biggest in its own state. Texans, eh?
2139 San Jacinto Boulevard

Texas Capitol
The state headquarters, however, still claims the title of the largest capitol in the USA, and anchors the north end of Congress Avenue.
See p026

The Independent
Out-of-kilter sections define this 209m tower, which became the city's tallest in 2019.
See p010

Seaholm Power Plant
A redevelopment finished in 2016 gave the late art deco power station, which started operation in 1948, a new lease of life and led to projects on nearby blocks (see p086).
800 W Cesar Chavez Street

Frost Bank Tower
Duda Paine's clever twist on Austin's heritage is perhaps Downtown's signature landmark.
See p012

One Eleven Congress
At 127m, the city's highest structure when it was inaugurated as One Congress Plaza in 1987, the pyramidical stepped storeys of this rebranded icon are lit in blue neon at night.
See p073

Lady Bird Lake
Formed by damming the Colorado River in 1960, the reservoir became an urban success story with the help of Lady Bird Johnson, who pushed for the beautification of its shores.

INTRODUCTION
THE CHANGING FACE OF THE URBAN SCENE

This is an ambitious city trying to sort out its identity. It is booming, but can give the impression that it still wants to be a sleepy, midsized town. It regularly tops lists of the USA's hippest destinations, yet you are as likely to see Stetsoned cowboys and pierced punks as smart entrepreneurs. And although a homegrown quirkiness is a point of pride, a tech boom and the affluence that came with it have turned the place more corporate than ever. Yet these incongruities are part of what makes the state capital such an interesting destination.

The visitor should bear in mind how much things have changed in so short a time. The population has leapt 70 per cent in a couple of decades, as tens of thousands arrive from Texas and beyond. The spurt remade entire neighbourhoods, reared a proper skyline and created a thriving culinary scene. Thankfully, fierce devotion to the local means independent businesses have profited, and old charms, such as its natural pools, have not been lost. Registering that Austin is feeling its way in the maelstrom of monumental change makes the brand of civic pride (which can be over the top) easier to handle.

Wherever the fortunes of Texas' fourth-largest city may lie, its people remain friendly, laidback and generous. A relaxed attitude is evident everywhere from barbecue joints to art galleries and fine-diners, and explains a great deal of the attraction. Here we give you a big headstart finding the inside track, and chances are high that you'll encounter a resident or two to lead you the rest of the way.

ESSENTIAL INFO
FACTS, FIGURES AND USEFUL ADDRESSES

TOURIST OFFICE
Austin Visitor Center
602 E 4th Street
T 512 478 0098
www.austintexas.org

TRANSPORT
Airport transfer to Downtown
Capital Metro Route 20 buses leave every 15 minutes (during regular service) from 5am to 11.30pm on weekdays, and 6am to 11.30pm at weekends. The journey takes about half an hour
www.capmetro.org/airport
Car hire
Silvercar
Austin-Bergstrom International Airport
T 512 666 9680
Taxis
Yellow Cab
T 512 452 9999
Travel card
A Capital Metro day pass costs $2.50
www.capmetro.org

EMERGENCY SERVICES
Emergencies
T 911
Police (non-emergencies)
T 311
24-hour pharmacy
Walgreens
6200 W William Cannon Drive
T 512 892 1933

CONSULATE GENERAL
British Consulate General
Suite 2400
1301 Fannin Street
Houston
T 713 210 4000
www.gov.uk/world/usa

POSTAL SERVICES
Post office
Suite 150, 823 Congress Avenue
T 800 275 8777
Shipping
UPS
Hilton hotel, 500 E 4th Street
T 512 682 2828

BOOKS
My Beautiful City Austin by David Heymann (John M Hardy Publishing Co)
Big Wonderful Thing: A History of Texas by Stephen Harrigan (University of Texas Press)

WEBSITES
Architecture
www.aiaaustin.org
Art
www.bigmedium.org
Newspaper
www.statesman.com

EVENTS
Art City Austin
www.artcityaustin.org
SXSW
www.sxsw.com

COST OF LIVING
Taxi from Austin-Bergstrom International Airport to city centre
$30
Cappuccino
$4.50
Packet of cigarettes
$7
Daily newspaper
$2
Bottle of champagne
$90

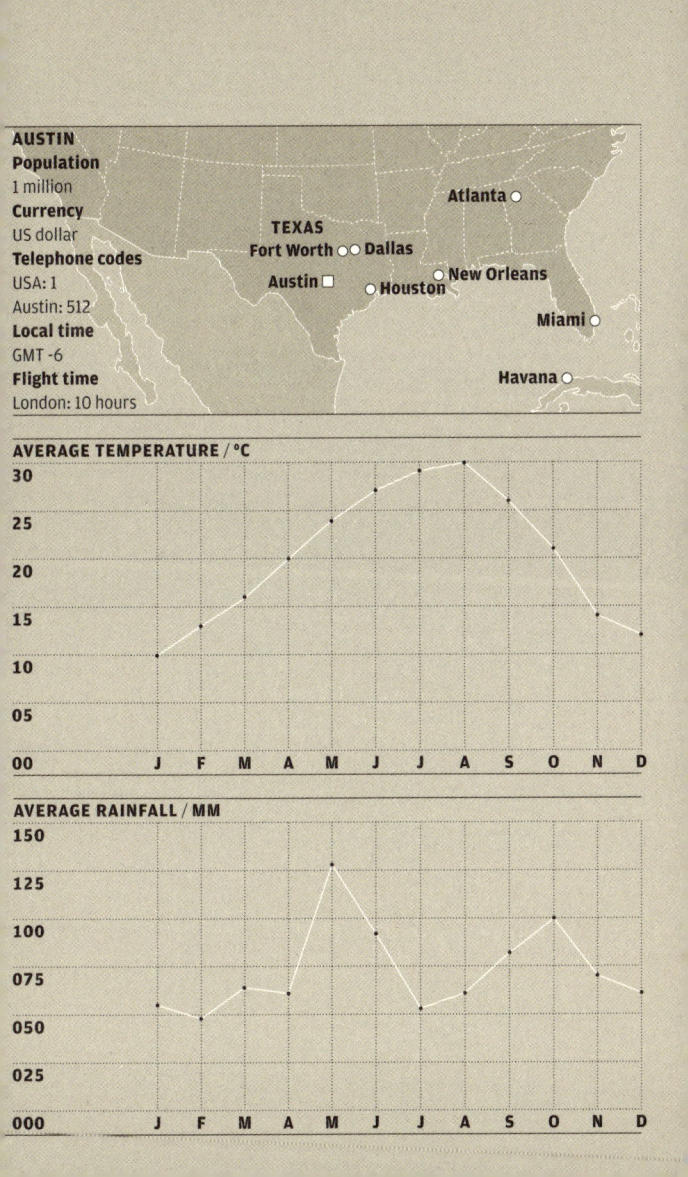

AUSTIN

Population
1 million
Currency
US dollar
Telephone codes
USA: 1
Austin: 512
Local time
GMT -6
Flight time
London: 10 hours

AVERAGE TEMPERATURE / °C

AVERAGE RAINFALL / MM

NEIGHBOURHOODS
THE AREAS YOU NEED TO KNOW AND WHY

To help you navigate the city, we've chosen the most interesting districts (see below and the map inside the back cover) and colour-coded our featured venues, according to their location; those venues that are outside these areas are not coloured.

DOWNTOWN
At the south end of Downtown, it's all about corporate business; in the north part, state government hums along near the Capitol (see p026). Apartments, office buildings and hotels (see p017) have moved in, but reminders of old Austin are preserved along Congress Avenue and E 6th Street.

CLARKSVILLE
Much of this slice of the city was built on the 1853 Woodlawn estate, whose main house still stands (1606 Niles Road). The district retains a residential character on its hilly, tree-lined streets – a contrast to the bustling shopping and dining corridors of N Lamar Boulevard and W 6th Street.

TRAVIS HEIGHTS
Pretty Travis Heights is a counterpoint to busy S Congress Avenue (see p088), which forms its western edge. It dates from the early 1900s, and the winding avenues are lined with handsome houses. The public spring-fed Big Stacy Pool (700 E Live Oak Street) attracts people from across town.

WAREHOUSE DISTRICT
The historic warehouses grouped around the former freight railway track have been repurposed. Now, pedestrian-friendly W 2nd Street is overshadowed by shiny condo and corporate towers. Quality restaurants including ATX Cocina (Suite 170, 110 San Antonio Street, T 512 263 2322) and She's Not Here (see p041) are major draws.

BOULDIN CREEK
Settled in the early 20th century – Mattie's (see p056) gives a glimpse of its pastoral beginnings – Bouldin Creek's renovated cottages and bungalows have real charm. Happening haunts (see p033) populate S Congress Avenue, while S 1st Street sports a mix of food trucks and offbeat shops.

EAST AUSTIN
Once considered the wrong side of town, the east has come good. Gentrification has transformed its gritty blocks, the best of which blend long-standing taquerias and watering holes with high-design eateries, buzzy hotels (see p018) and fashion stores such as House of St Clair (see p092).

ZILKER
There are plenty of restaurants (see p057) and hip boutiques (see p088) on S Lamar Boulevard and Barton Springs Road, but Zilker is most popular for its large park, a year-round festival ground. Within it, the Umlauf Sculpture Garden & Museum (see p064) displays the work of the local artist.

UNIVERSITY/WEST CAMPUS
The massive University of Texas (see p014) defines the area to the north of Downtown. Venture into the campus to discover its impressive art collection (see p074) and the LBJ Presidential Library (see p084). Bypass the studenty hangouts around its edges in favour of bistro Goodall's in Hotel Ella (see p016), a restored 1900 estate.

LANDMARKS
THE SHAPE OF THE CITY SKYLINE

Austin has always been defined by geography. The city was laid out in 1839 along the Colorado River, where the blackland prairie meets the rocky Hill Country (see p096). Surveyor Edwin Waller devised the early street grid between two creeks, Waller and Shoal, and as development escalated this extended further and further afield. Previously, the more desirable districts were situated to the north and the west, whereas the poorer neighbourhoods lay east of Downtown. Rapid ongoing gentrification has changed all that, and once-neglected East Austin is now a sought-after locale.

Two key landmarks, the 1888 Capitol (see p026) and the 1937 University of Texas Tower (see p014), both perched on hills, have dominated the horizon for eons. They are still easy to spot, but a rising skyline is giving them serious competition. Construction of the Westgate Tower (see p011) in 1966 prompted the adoption of 'view corridors' to protect sightlines, controlling the placement of skyscrapers like the 56-floor The Austonian (200 Congress Avenue) and The Independent (see p010). As growth continues, concerns about how new projects integrate with older architecture intensify, especially in formerly low-density areas. Meanwhile, it's laudable that historic structures, including the Moonlight Towers (see p015), have been preserved. Ideally, future schemes will retain some of the scale and charm that makes this such an appealing destination.
For full addresses, see Resources.

The Independent

Recent development has led to a drastic reshaping of the formerly low-rise district around Seaholm Power Plant (800 W Cesar Chavez Street), itself reborn as a mixed-use office/retail complex. In a far cry from the area's gritty past, the old warehouses have given way to luxury condominium towers. The most prominent of these is the 209m The Independent, which became Austin's tallest building on its completion in 2019. Local architects Rhode Partners gave it a distinctive profile by offsetting groups of floors. While the effect perhaps lacks the complexity and elegance of other 'Jenga' towers around the world, it is a welcome departure from the cookie-cutter design of nearby blocks. Its mesh crown encloses structural bracing and a giant water tank that help combat sway in strong winds.
301 West Avenue

Westgate Tower

Considering the current upwards trajectory of the city, it's easy to forget that this now relatively modest skyscraper drew fire for its height. And yet the 80m Westgate Tower did just that in the early 1960s, prompting the Texas legislature to try (and narrowly fail) to block its construction. The primary objection was the sensitive location, on the western border of the Capitol (see p026), hence its moniker, which officials deemed an 'encroachment of commercialism' on a symbol of the state. But since its unveiling in 1966, it has come to be appreciated as an exemplar of midcentury style. This is due to revered New York architect Edward Durell Stone's design, which melds delicate brick latticework with ranks of balconies in a way that manages to emphasise the building's height while downplaying its presence.
1122 Colorado Street

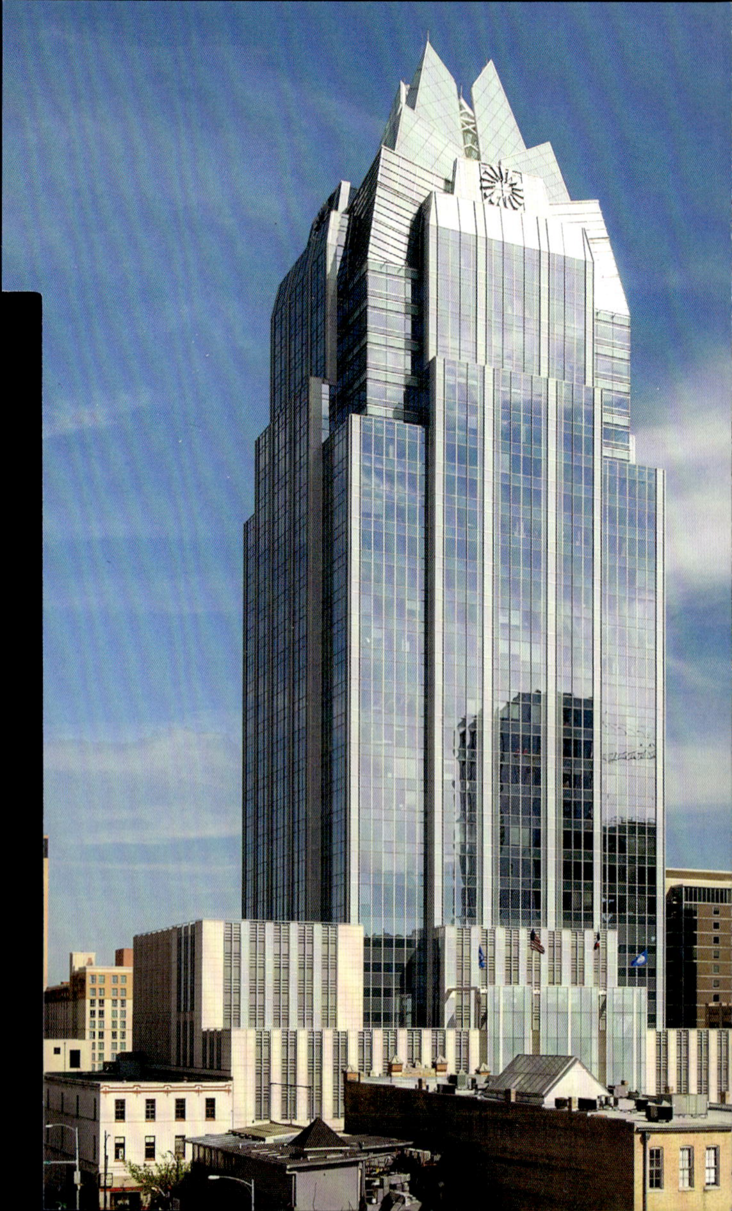

AUSTIN
A COLOUR-CODED GUIDE TO THE HOT 'HOODS

DOWNTOWN
Suits, students and state workers mingle in Austin's bustling financial and political heart

CLARKSVILLE
A thriving retail and restaurant scene brings people to this pleasant and pretty suburb

TRAVIS HEIGHTS
Low-key charm prevails in a desirable residential district south of the Colorado River

WAREHOUSE DISTRICT
Swanky apartments, office blocks and eateries oil the wheels of the former industrial zone

BOULDIN CREEK
Singular shops and hip cafés are peppered among attractive turn-of-the-century houses

EAST AUSTIN
Its once tired and neglected streets are now lined with boutiques and creative ventures

ZILKER
A stone's throw from Downtown, the parkland and greenery here offer an urban escape

UNIVERSITY/WEST CAMPUS
The city's sprawling academic hub encompasses some key cultural and sporting venues

For a full description of each neighbourhood, see the Introduction.
Featured venues are colour-coded, according to the district in which they are located.

PHOTOGRAPHERS

Lisa Petrole
The Independent, p010
Kimpton Van Zandt, p017
The Carpenter Hotel, p019
South Congress Hotel, p020, p021
The Contemporary Austin, p028, p029
Lady Bird Lake Trail Restroom, p031
Joann's Fine Foods, p032, p033
Mohawk, p037
Comedor, p038
Garage, p039
She's Not Here, p041
Arlo Grey, p042
Greater Goods, p044, p045
Ellis, pp048-049
Easy Tiger, p053
Bar Peached, p054, p055
Barley Swine, p060
Ty Haney, p063
Mystic Raven, p065
One Eleven Congress, p073
City Hall, p079
Keith Kreeger Studios, p091
House of St Clair, pp092-093
Esby, p095

Wade Griffith
Westgate Tower, p011
Frost Bank Tower, pp012-013
The University of Texas Main Building, p014
Moonlight Towers, p015
Heywood Hotel, p018
Hotel Saint Cecilia, p022
Hillside Farmacy, p025
Texas Capitol, pp026-027
ESB-MACC, p030
Deep Eddy Pool, p035
Milk + Honey, p036
Lucy's Fried Chicken, p046
Jeffrey's, p050
Contigo, pp058-059
Lamberts Downtown Barbecue, p061
St Martin's Ev Lutheran Church, p078
The East Village, pp080-081
Circuit of the Americas, p082
St Edward's Residential Village, p083
LBJ Presidential Library, p084, p085
Salt & Time, p094
John F Kennedy Memorial, p099

Richard Barnes
Menil Drawing Institute, pp100-101

Blanton Museum of Art
Austin by Ellsworth Kelly, p074, p075

Andrea Calo
Mass Gallery, pp068-069

Ryann Ford
Juniper, p047

Nicole Franzen
Hotel Emma, p098

Jim Innes
Austin city view, inside front cover

Graeber Jolly
Grayduck Gallery, p066

Judd Foundation/VAGA, NY/DACS
The Chinati Foundation, p102

Sarah Frankie Linder
Big Medium, p071

Jim Parsons
United States Courthouse, pp076-077

WALLPAPER* CITY GUIDES

Executive Editor
Jeremy Case

Author
Jim Parsons

Photography Editor
Rebecca Moldenhauer

Art Editor
Jade R Arroyo

Senior Sub-Editor
Sean McGeady

Editorial Assistant
Josh Lee

Contributors
Lindsey Derrington
Matt Johns
Charles Peveto
Rob Silver

Interns
Alison Evans
Rashida Jasdanwalla
Anqi La
Alex Merola

Austin Imprint
First published 2014
Second edition 2020

ISBN 978 1 83866 045 1

More City Guides
www.phaidon.com/travel

Follow us
@wallpaperguides

Contact
wcg@phaidon.com

Original Design
Loran Stosskopf

Map Illustrator
Russell Bell

Production Controller
Gif Jittiwutikarn

Assistant Production Controller
Lily Rodgers

Wallpaper* Magazine
161 Marsh Wall
London E14 9AP
contact@wallpaper.com

Wallpaper*® is a registered trademark of TI Media

Phaidon Press Limited
Regent's Wharf
All Saints Street
London N1 9PA

Phaidon Press Inc
65 Bleecker Street
New York, NY 10012

All prices and venue information are correct at time of going to press, but are subject to change.

A CIP Catalogue record for this book is available from the British Library.

All rights reserved. No part of this publication may be reproduced, stored in a retrieval system or transmitted, in any form or by any means, electronic, mechanical, photocopying, recording or otherwise, without the prior permission of Phaidon Press.

Phaidon® is a registered trademark of Phaidon Press Limited

© Phaidon Press Limited

Hotel Magdalena 016
Room rates:
prices on request
1101 Music Lane
T 512 442 1000
www.hotelmagdalena.com

Proper 016
Room rates:
prices on request
600 W 2nd Street
T 512 628 1500
www.properhotel.com/hotels/austin

Hotel Saint Cecilia 022
Room rates:
double, from $290
112 Academy Drive
T 512 852 2400
www.hotelsaintcecilia.com

Hotel St George 096
Room rates:
double, from $150
105 S Highland Avenue
Marfa
T 432 729 3700
www.marfasaintgeorge.com

Hotel San José 016
Room rates:
double, from $270
1316 S Congress Avenue
T 512 852 2350
www.sanjosehotel.com

South Congress Hotel 020
Room rates:
double, from $220;
Milton suite, from $1,000
1603 S Congress Avenue
T 512 920 6405
www.southcongresshotel.com

HOTELS
ADDRESSES AND ROOM RATES

Arrive East Austin 016
Room rates:
double, from $150
1813 E 6th Street
T 512 399 1927
www.arrivehotels.com

The Carpenter Hotel 019
Room rates:
double, from $270;
Large King, from $290
400 Josephine Street
T 512 682 5300
www.carpenterhotel.com

Contigo Ranch 097
Room rates:
cottage, from $150;
cabin, from $200
two-night minimum stay
13454 Lower Crabapple Road
Fredericksburg
T 830 685 3464
www.contigoranchfredericksburg.com

The Driskill 072
Room rates:
double, from $380
604 Brazos Street
T 512 439 1234
www.driskillhotel.com

Hotel Ella 016
Room rates:
double, from $250
1900 Rio Grande Street
T 512 495 1800
www.hotelella.com

Hotel Emma 098
Room rates:
double, from $350
136 E Grayson Street
San Antonio
T 210 448 8300
www.thehotelemma.com

Heywood Hotel 018
Room rates:
double, from $200;
King Patio, from $260
1609 E Cesar Chavez Street
T 512 271 5522
www.heywoodhotel.com

The Joule 099
Room rates:
double, from $260
1530 Main Street
Dallas
T 214 748 1300
www.thejouledallas.com

Kimber Modern 023
Room rates:
double, from $200;
White Suite, from $400
110 The Circle
T 512 985 9990
www.kimbermodern.com

Kimpton Hotel Van Zandt 017
Room rates:
double, from $300;
spa suite, from $350
605 Davis Street
T 512 542 5300
www.hotelvanzandt.com

United States Courthouse 076
 501 W 5th Street
The University of Texas Main Building 014
 110 Inner Campus Drive
 T 512 475 6636
 www.utexas.edu

W
Wally Workman 064
 1202 W 6th Street
 T 512 472 7428
 www.wallyworkmangallery.com
Waterloo Records 088
 600 N Lamar Boulevard
 T 512 474 2500
 www.waterloorecords.com
Westgate Tower 011
 1122 Colorado Street
The White Horse 040
 500 Comal Street
 T 512 553 6756
 www.thewhitehorseaustin.com
Wink Restaurant & Wine Bar 040
 1014 N Lamar Boulevard
 T 512 482 8868
 www.winkrestaurant.com

Salt & Time 094
1912 E 7th Street
T 512 524 1383
www.saltandtime.com

Scarbrough Building 072
101 W 6th Street

Sculpture Falls 035
1710 Camp Craft Road
Barton Creek Wilderness Park

Seaholm Power Plant 010
800 W Cesar Chavez Street

She's Not Here 041
440 W 2nd Street
T 512 888 1970
www.snhaustin.com

Signor Vineyards 097
362 Livesay Lane
Fredericksburg
T 830 304 7446
www.signorvineyards.com

The Sixth Floor Museum 099
411 Elm Street
Dallas
T 214 747 6660
www.jfk.org

Springdale General 088
1023 Springdale Road
T 512 416 1234
www.springdalegeneral.com

Stag 088
1423 S Congress Avenue
T 512 373 7824
www.stagprovisions.com

Stubb's 024
801 Red River Street
T 512 480 8341
www.stubbsaustin.com

Suerte 051
1800 E 6th Street
T 512 953 0092
www.suerteatx.com
Dinner and weekend brunch only

T
Tecovas 034
1333 S Congress Avenue
T 512 675 4343
www.tecovas.com

Texas Capitol 026
112 E 11th Street
T 512 305 8400
www.tspb.texas.gov

Texas Hillel: The Topfer Center for Jewish Life 072
2105 San Antonio Street

U
UB Preserv 100
1609 Westheimer
Houston
T 346 406 5923
www.ubpreserv.com

Uchi 040
801 S Lamar Boulevard
T 512 916 4808
www.uchiaustin.com

Umlauf Sculpture Garden & Museum 064
605 Azie Morton Road
T 512 445 5582
www.umlaufsculpture.org

Mystic Raven 065
*Lamar Boulevard/W 29th Street
Pease Park
www.peasepark.org*

N

NASA Johnson Space Center 096
*2nd Street/Saturn Lane
Houston
T 281 244 2100
www.nasa.gov*
Native Bar & Kitchen 040
*807 E 4th Street
T 512 551 9947
www.nativehostels.com/bar*
Noah Marion 088
*2053 S Lamar Boulevard
T 512 981 6692
www.noahmarion.com*
Northern-Southern 064
*1900b E 12th Street
www.northern-southern.com*
Norwood Tower 072
114 W 7th Street

O

Olamaie 040
*1610 San Antonio Street
T 512 474 2796
www.olamaieaustin.com*
One Eleven Congress 073
*111 Congress Avenue
www.111congressave.com*
Outdoor Voices 062
*606 Blanco Street
T 512 356 9136
www.outdoorvoices.com*

P
P6 042
*Line
111 E Cesar Chavez Street
T 512 473 1566
www.thelinehotel.com*
Parkside 024
*301 E 6th Street
T 512 474 9898
www.parkside-austin.com*
Peached Tortilla 055
*Suite 100
5520 Burnet Road
T 512 330 4439
www.thepeachedtortilla.com*
Petrified Design 064
www.petrifieddesign.com
Pool Burger 024
*2315 Lake Austin Boulevard
T 512 334 9747
www.poolburger.com*

R
Ruby City 098
*150 Camp Street
San Antonio
T 210 226 6663
www.rubycity.org*

S
St Edward's Residential Village 083
*3001 S Congress Avenue
www.stedwards.edu*
St Martin's Ev Lutheran Church 078
*606 W 15th Street
T 512 476 6757
www.saintmartins.org*

Lisa Crowder 088
*Suite 102
Building 3
Canopy
916 Springdale Road
T 512 524 0364
www.lisacrowder.com*
Lora Reynolds Gallery 070
*Suite 50
360 Nueces Street
T 512 215 4965
www.lorareynolds.com*
Loro 057
*2115 S Lamar Boulevard
T 512 916 4858
www.loroaustin.com*
Lucy's Fried Chicken 046
*2218 College Avenue
T 512 297 2423
www.lucysfriedchicken.com*

M
Made by Eliana 088
*Building 6F
Springdale General
1023 Springdale Road
www.elianabernard.com*
Mass Gallery 068
*705 Gunter Street
T 512 535 4946
www.massgallery.org*
Mattie's 056
*Green Pastures
811 W Live Oak Street
T 512 444 1888
www.mattiesaustin.com*

Maudie's 062
*2608 W 7th Street
T 512 473 3740
www.maudies.com*
Maufrais 088
*1512 S Congress Avenue
T 512 945 9905
maufrais.shop*
The Menil Collection 100
*1533 Sul Ross Street
Houston
T 713 525 9400
www.menil.org*
Menil Drawing Institute 100
*1412 W Main Street
Houston
T 713 525 9400
www.menil.org*
Mexic-Arte Museum 030
*419 Congress Avenue
T 512 480 9373
www.mexic-artemuseum.org*
Milk + Honey 036
*100a Guadalupe Street
T 512 236 1115
www.milkandhoneyspa.com*
Miranda Bennett Studio 088
*1211 E 11th Street
T 512 432 5121
www.shopmirandabennett.com*
Mohawk 037
*912 Red River Street
T 512 666 0877
www.mohawkaustin.com*
Moonlight Tower 015
Lydia Street/E 11th Street

House of St Clair 092
1905 E 12th Street
T 512 551 9515
www.houseofstclair.com

I
ICOSA 064
Suite 102
Building 2
Canopy
916 Springdale Road
T 512 920 2062
www.icosacollective.com
The Independent 010
301 West Avenue

J
Jeffrey's 050
1204 W Lynn Street
T 512 477 5584
www.jeffreysofaustin.com
Joann's Fine Foods 032
1224 S Congress Avenue
T 512 358 6054
www.joannsaustin.com
John F Kennedy Memorial Plaza 099
646 Main Street
Dallas
www.jfk.org
June's All Day 062
1722 S Congress Avenue
T 512 416 1722
www.junesallday.com
Juniper 047
Suite 304
2400 E Cesar Chavez Street
T 512 220 9421
www.juniperaustin.com

Justine's 062
4710 E 5th Street
T 512 385 2900
www.justines1937.com

K
Keith Kreeger Studios 091
Suite 104
Building 3
Canopy
916 Springdale Road
www.keithkreeger.com
Kemuri Tatsu-ya 040
2713 E 2nd Street
T 512 893 5561
www.kemuri-tatsuya.com
Kick Pleat 062
624 N Lamar Boulevard
T 512 445 4500
www.kickpleat.com
Kimbell Art Museum 096
3333 Camp Bowie Boulevard
Fort Worth
T 817 332 8451
www.kimbellart.org

L
Lady Bird Lake Trail Restroom 031
Rainey Street/Cummings Street
Lamberts Downtown Barbecue 061
401 W 2nd Street
T 512 494 1500
www.lambertsaustin.com
LBJ Presidential Library 084
2313 Red River Street
T 512 721 0200
www.lbjlibrary.org
LeRoy and Lewis Barbecue 040
121 Pickle Road
www.leroyandlewis.com

Eberly 052
615 S Lamar Boulevard
T 512 916 9000
www.eberlyaustin.com

Elisabet Ney Museum 064
304 E 44th Street
T 512 974 1625
www.austintexas.gov/elisabetney

Eliza Page 090
229 W 2nd Street
T 512 474 6500
www.elizapage.com

Ellis 048
Building 2
111 Congress Avenue
www.ellisofaustin.com

Emo's 062
2015 E Riverside Drive
T 888 512 7469
www.emosaustin.com

ESB-MACC 030
600 River Street
T 512 974 3772
www.austintexas.gov/esbmacc

Esby 095
1601 S 1st Street
T 512 243 8901
www.esbyapparel.com

F
Feathers 062
1700b S Congress Avenue
T 512 912 9779
www.feathersboutiquevintage.com

Frost Bank Tower 012
401 Congress Avenue

G
Garage 039
503 Colorado Street
T 512 369 3490
www.garagetx.com

Governor's Mansion 072
1010 Colorado Street
T 512 305 8524
www.tspb.texas.gov

Grayduck Gallery 066
2213 E Cesar Chavez Street
T 512 826 5334
www.grayduckgallery.com

Greater Goods Coffee Roasters 044
2501 E 5th Street
T 512 382 9857
www.greatergoodsroasting.com

H
Half Step 040
7512 Rainey Street
T 512 391 1877
www.halfstepbar.com

Helm 088
Suite 101
1200 E 11th Street
T 512 609 8150
www.helmboots.com

Herbert Bohn House 072
1301 W 29th Street

Hillside Farmacy 025
1209 E 11th Street
T 512 628 0168
www.hillsidefarmacy.com

Houndstooth Coffee 043
Suite 101
2823 E Martin Luther King Jr Boulevard
T 512 243 8902
www.houndstoothcoffee.com

Canopy 064
916 Springdale Road
T 512 939 6665
www.canopyaustin.com

The Capri 103
601 W San Antonio Street
Thunderbird Hotel
Marfa
T 432 729 1984
www.thunderbirdmarfa.com

The Chinati Foundation 103
1 Cavalry Row
Marfa
T 432 729 4362
www.chinati.org

Circuit of the Americas 082
9201 Circuit of the Americas Boulevard
T 512 301 6600
www.circuitoftheamericas.com

City Hall 079
301 W 2nd Street
T 512 974 2000
www.austintexas.gov

Comedor 038
501 Colorado Street
T 512 499 0977
www.comedortx.com

The Contemporary Austin at Jones Center 028
700 Congress Avenue
T 512 453 5312
www.thecontemporaryaustin.org

The Contemporary Austin at Laguna Gloria 028
3809 W 35th Street
T 512 458 8191
www.thecontemporaryaustin.org

Contigo 058
2027 Anchor Lane
T 512 614 2260
www.contigotexas.com/restaurant
Dinner and Sunday brunch only

The Continental Club 062
1315 S Congress Avenue
T 512 441 2444
www.continentalclub.com

D

Deep Eddy Cabaret 062
2315 Lake Austin Boulevard
T 512 472 0961
www.deepeddycabaret.com

Deep Eddy Pool 035
401 Deep Eddy Drive
T 512 472 8546
www.austintexas.gov/department/deep-eddy-pool

Desert Door Texas Sotol Distillery 089
211 Darden Hill Road
Driftwood
T 512 829 6129
www.desertdoor.com

Domo Alley-Gato 024
1600 E 6th Street
T 512 893 5561
www.domo-tatsuya.com

Dry Creek Cafe 062
4812 Mount Bonnell Road
T 512 453 9244

E

The East Village 080
1200 E 11th Street

Easy Tiger 053
709 E 6th Street
T 512 614 4972
www.easytigerusa.com

RESOURCES
CITY GUIDE DIRECTORY

A

The Alamo 096
300 Alamo Plaza
San Antonio
T 210 225 1391
www.thealamo.org

Allen's Boots 034
1522 S Congress Avenue
T 512 447 1413
www.allensboots.com

Antone's 062
305 E 5th Street
T 512 814 0361
www.antonesnightclub.com

Arlo Grey 042
111 E Cesar Chavez Street
Line
T 512 478 2991
www.thelinehotel.com

Austin Central Library 086
710 W Cesar Chavez Street
T 512 974 7400
www.library.austintexas.gov/central-library

Austin by Ellsworth Kelly 074
200 E Martin Luther King Jr Boulevard
T 512 471 7324
www.blantonmuseum.org/ellsworth-kellys-austin

Austin Federal Courthouse 076
200 W 8th Street

The Austonian 009
200 Congress Avenue

B

Ballroom 096
108 E San Antonio Street
Marfa
T 432 729 3600
www.ballroommarfa.org

Bar Peached 054
1315 W 6th Street
T 512 992 0666
www.barpeached.com
Dinner and Sunday brunch only

La Barbecue 018
2027 E Cesar Chavez Street
www.labarbecue.com

Barley Swine 060
Suite 400
6555 Burnet Road
T 512 394 8150
www.barleyswine.com

Barton Springs Pool 062
2131 William Barton Drive
T 512 974 6300
www.austintexas.gov/pools

Big Medium 071
Suite 101
Building 2
Canopy
916 Springdale Road
T 512 939 6665
www.bigmedium.org

Brandon Mike 067
www.brandonmike.com

Bufalina 018
1519 E Cesar Chavez Street
T 512 524 2523
www.bufalinapizza.com

By George 067
1400 S Congress Avenue
524 N Lamar Boulevard
T 512 441 8600
www.bygeorgeaustin.com

C

Canoe 088
www.canoegoods.com

NOTES
SKETCHES AND MEMOS

Wallpaper*
City Guide

50 CITIES NOW AVAILABLE IN ONE APP

Your passport to global style
Download digital guides for Android and Apple phones and tablets in one container app via
www.phaidon.com/wcg

Marfa

For its first century, Marfa was little more than a dusty backroad. Then came Donald Judd. The minimalist artist relocated from New York in the 1970s, drawn by the desert landscape and quality of light. He turned an old military compound into The Chinati Foundation (T 432 729 4362; opposite), a setting for his own large-scale works, and those of his peers, including Richard Long, Dan Flavin and Claes Oldenburg and Coosje van Bruggen. This was the catalyst for the arrival of further galleries and standalone installations such as Elmgreen & Dragset's surreal *Prada Marfa* beside US Highway 90. There's a culinary scene too, headlined by Rocky Barnette's homage to Chihuahuan tradition – his dishes might feature rabbit, grasshopper, prickly pear or mesquite – in The Capri (T 432 729 1984; above), part of the renovated 1950s Thunderbird Hotel.

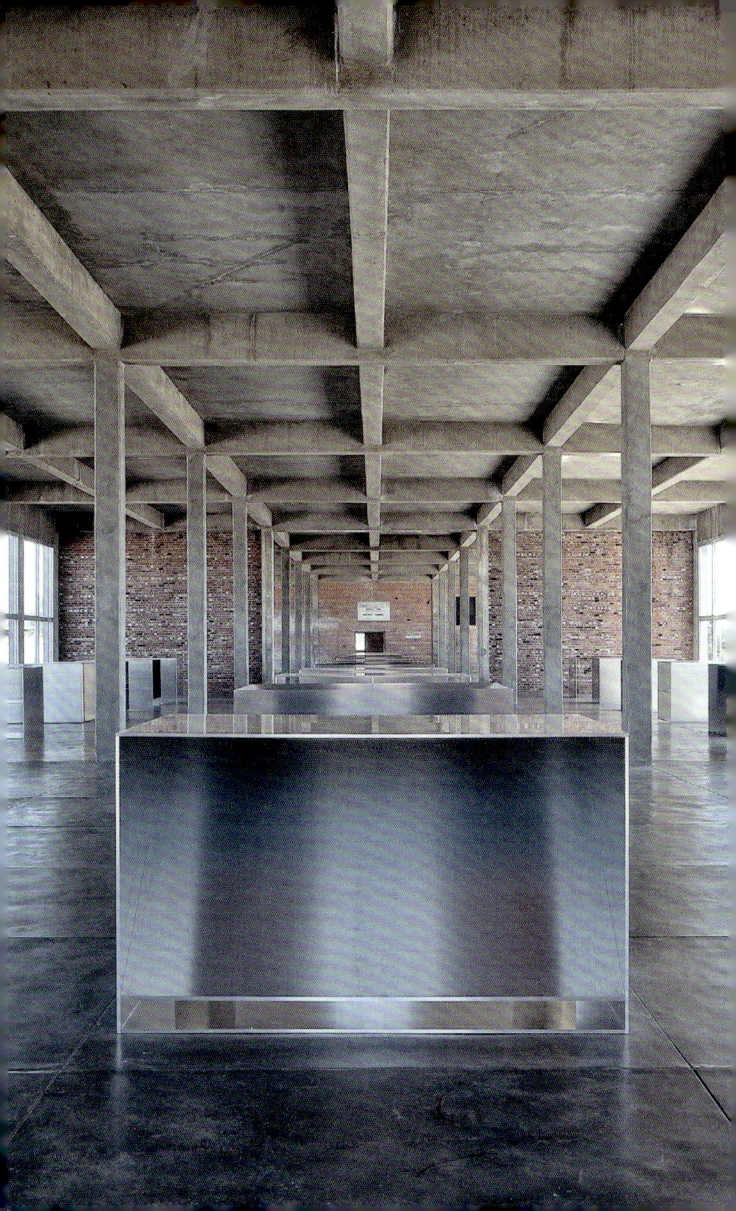

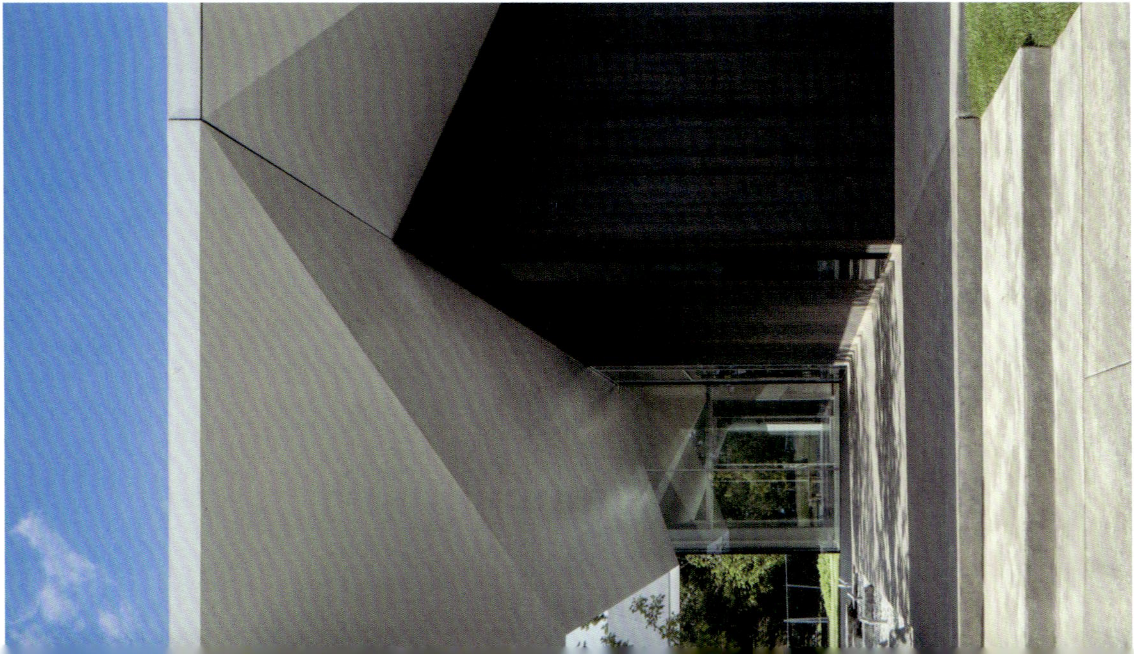

Menil Drawing Institute, Houston
Texas' largest city can seem intimidating: a tangle of freeways, strip malls and glassy skyscrapers sprawls in every direction. We advise you focus on neighbourhoods such as leafy Montrose, in which you'll find The Menil Collection (1533 Sul Ross Street), an art museum in a classic 1987 Renzo Piano building, and the Menil Drawing Institute (right), which houses nearly 2,000 pieces with a focus on 19th-century modernism, Cubism, surrealism and expressionism; it also hosts touring exhibitions. Designed by Johnston Marklee and opened in 2018, it's a serene series of low-lying structures, clad in cedar planks or glazed, and tied together by a steel-plate roof. Nearby, the arresting Rothko Chapel features his final 14-painting cycle. Book for dinner at UB Preserv (T 346 406 5923), which deftly melds South Asian, Mexican, Creole and southern US flavours.
1412 W Main Street, T 713 525 9400, www.menil.org

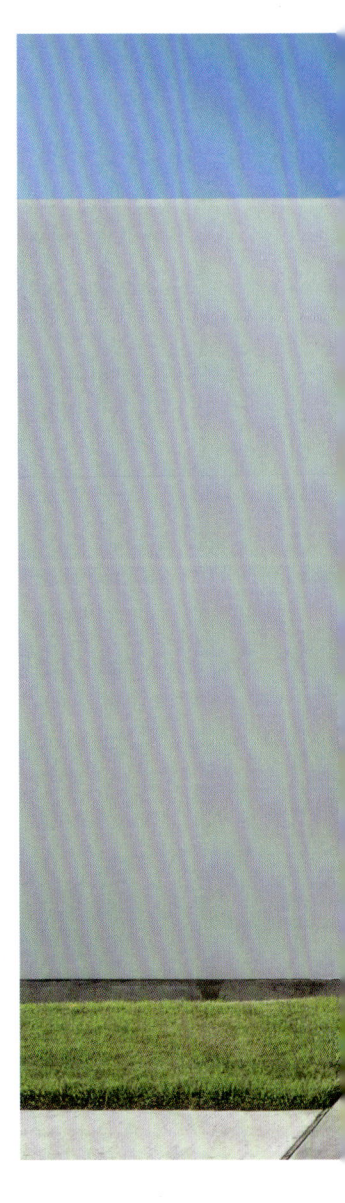

John F Kennedy Memorial Plaza, Dallas
The long-running 1978 TV series gave Dallas its larger-than-life reputation and, in many ways, 'Big D' stands up to the legend. This is, after all, a city built on oil fortunes. So act like a tycoon and book into slick hotel The Joule (T 214 748 1300), with interiors by Adam Tihany and a pool that cantilevers out over Main Street. Then visit Fair Park, the showcase for Texas' centenary in 1936 comprising one of the largest collections of art deco expo architecture in the world. But the city's headline draw is Dealey Plaza, the site of the 1963 JFK assassination. The Sixth Floor Museum (T 214 747 6660) chronicles the shooting itself. Two blocks away is the memorial, erected in 1970. Philip Johnson's design is brilliant in its simplicity: an open-air square 'room' with stilted concrete walls encircling a simple slab of black granite.
646 Main Street, www.jfk.org

Hotel Emma, San Antonio

San Antonio's Spanish colonial history has long been a draw. But it has recently come into its own as a happening contemporary destination due to projects including the redevelopment of the 1894 Pearl Brewery, with Hotel Emma at its heart. Designed by Roman and Williams, nods to the past are everywhere, from an ammonia compressor painted red and repurposed as lobby art to booths made from cast-iron fermentation tanks in the bar (above), while 146 rooms have old-world elements like rustic leather seating and bathrooms clad in handmade tiles. Venture out beyond the beaten track to investigate the vibrant mural scene and David Adjaye's dramatic deep-red Ruby City (T 210 226 6663), opened in 2019 to show Linda Pace's superb hoard of postwar art. *136 E Grayson Street, T 210 448 8300, www.thehotelemma.com*

Contigo Ranch, Fredericksburg
Ranching scion Frede Edgerton and wife Claudia commissioned architects Design Hound to transform a series of Hill Country buildings into four cabins and 10 cottages, which opened as a tranquil retreat in 2017. Interiors by daughter-in-law Ann Edgerton exude a modern rustic charm, and antique rugs and chairs have been complemented with pieces from Austin makers including furniture by Brian Chilton and tapestries by Hallie Lauren Brewer. There's no restaurant but breakfast baskets are delivered each morning, and the town of Fredericksburg is a short drive away. Spend the day visiting any of more than 50 wineries in the area, mainly specialising in merlot and cabernet sauvignon – Signor Vineyards (T 830 304 7446) is one of the most picturesque.
13454 Lower Crabapple Road, T 830 685 3464, www.contigoranchfredericksburg.com

ESCAPES

WHERE TO GO IF YOU WANT TO LEAVE TOWN

For a day trip, it's hard to beat the Texas Hill Country. A short drive west, the region is known for its gorgeous landscapes and quaint towns. Take in the natural beauty at Pedernales Falls, and head to Luckenbach to catch live country and bluegrass music in an 1887 dancehall at weekends; base yourself at Contigo Ranch (opposite).

Although the state is vast, Austin is located in the centre, so most destinations are a fairly easy reach. It is a 90-minute sojourn south to San Antonio (see p098), where the River Walk meanders past museums, picturesque neighbourhoods and Spanish missions – the city was established in 1718 around San Antonio de Valero, better known as The Alamo (300 Alamo Plaza, T 210 225 1391), the site of the legendary 1836 seige and subsequent defeat by the Mexicans. And it is three hours to either Dallas (see p099) or Houston, to see the Menil Drawing Institute and Collection (see p100) and to ogle a rocket that took man to the moon at the NASA Johnson Space Center (2nd Street/Saturn Lane, T 281 244 2100). In neighbouring Fort Worth, the Kimbell Art Museum (3333 Camp Bowie Boulevard, T 817 332 8451) is housed in a landmark Louis Kahn building.

It's also well worth the trek – six-and-a-half hours by car, or three from El Paso airport – to Marfa for world-class art at Chinati (see p102) and Ballroom (108 E San Antonio Street, T 432 729 3600). Stay at stylish Hotel St George (105 S Highland Avenue, T 432 729 3700). *For full addresses, see Resources.*

Esby

Stephanie Beard's womenswear and unisex label of versatile basics prioritises ethical and sustainable practices and durable all-natural materials. Earth tones predominate in pieces such as loose-fitting French terry trousers in a subtle herringbone pattern, light linen shirts, and the signature belted, wide-legged 'Savannah Jumpsuit'. There's an emphasis on US-made items, including an Esby range of leather and suede totes and purses. It also stocks Freda Salvador footwear, Krewe shades and Blanca Monrós Gómez jewellery. The boutique was once a garage, transformed by local Duffy Stone, who whitewashed the walls and high wood ceilings, repurposed the old cinderblocks, and brought in thrift furniture and birch shelves. Roll-up glass doors face the street.
1601 S 1st Street, T 512 243 8901,
www.esbyapparel.com

Salt & Time

You wouldn't expect a charcuterie business owner to have spent almost a decade as a vegan. But Ben Runkle did just that, before realising it wasn't the meat per se that was troubling him, but rather the processing and the factory-farming. After studying in California, he launched in Austin, ordering the produce directly from sustainably run ranches across the state. In 2013, he allied with butcher Bryan Butler to create Salt & Time, with an industrial interior devised by Runkle's wife, Natalie Davis. Come to taste the locally famous steaks and salumi; four types of Texas cheese; wine from Southold Farm + Cellar; and delicatessen items from further afield, such as tinned fish by José Gourmet in Portugal. The restaurant opens for lunch, dinner and weekend brunch.
1912 E 7th Street, T 512 524 1383,
www.saltandtime.com

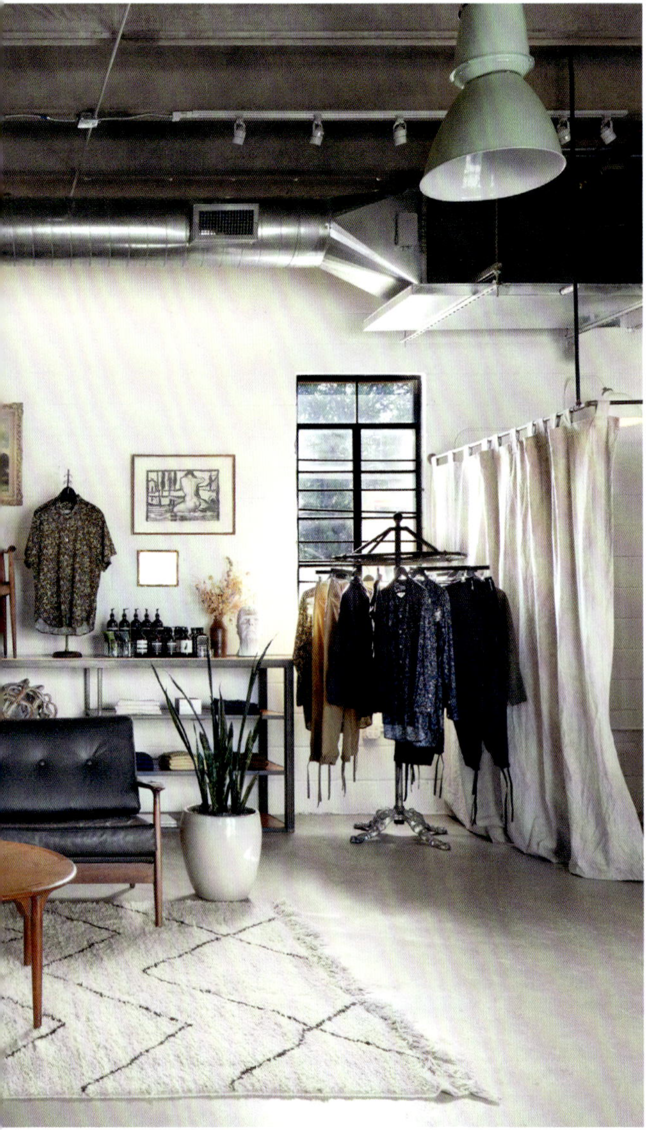

House of St Clair

Beautifully presented in a handsome gas station conversion, Carson Monahan and Lauren Kirby's menswear has roots in the 1940s and 1950s but brings in elements of streetwear and grunge, in pieces such as ripstop anoraks, wide-leg chambray trousers, and a military-inspired velvet overshirt. There's in-house jewellery too, and the art, decor and books are for sale.
1905 E 12th Street, T 512 551 9515

Keith Kreeger Studios

New Yorker Keith Kreeger was headed for a law career when a university ceramics class changed his course. He founded a studio on Cape Cod, moved here in 2009 and now his tableware graces more than 40 venues across the country, among them Uchi and Olamaie (see p040) and Salt & Time (see p094) in Austin. It is obvious to see why, as the breezy, sketch-like linear patterns coordinate easily across plates, bowls and platters, and slot into most surroundings. Signed hand-thrown items include lovely pastel-glazed vases and rustic pitchers. In his store in the Canopy complex (see p064), they're displayed on custom modules from locals Ankor Studios and Jobe Fabrications under Kreeger's porcelain pendant lighting. Open Wednesday to Friday, 11am to 5pm. *Suite 104, Building 3, 916 Springdale Road, www.keithkreeger.com*

Eliza Page

Jewellery guru Elizabeth Gibson's boutique in the heart of the 2nd Street retail district has been a go-to since 2005. The focus is on hand-finishing, and accompanying each piece are details on its maker's background. The store promotes artisans from Austin and Texas (and lesser-known national and foreign creatives) including Shaesby Scott, who produces delightfully sculptural items, and Jen Leddy, whose exquisite one-offs feature recycled materials. Gibson trained in metalsmithing and lost-wax casting, and her work ranges from minimal pendants to intricate art deco-inspired gemstone rings. Architect Kevin Gallaugher and designer Kasey McCarty's showroom boasts polished concrete floors, bespoke walnut cabinetry and quirky furniture like the velvet poufs.
229 W 2nd Street, T 512 474 6500,
www.elizapage.com

Desert Door Texas Sotol
Spirits made from the evergreen sotol, a spiky desert plant that typically grows wild in northern Mexico and south-west Texas, are common over the border but relatively unknown in the US. Ryan Campbell, Judson Kauffman and Brent Looby started Desert Door in 2017 to change that. The distillery in Driftwood turns sotol harvested from ranches near Fort Stockton and Iraan into two varieties of liquor: a citrusy, herbal, slightly sweet original, which can be sipped straight or swapped for vodka, tequila or gin in a cocktail, and a warmer, spicier oak-aged version reminiscent of bourbon. The bottles are coloured in deep blue and gold or silver – hues that evoke the local sunset. To find out more, it is a half-hour drive to the HQ (T 512 829 6129), which offers tours and tastings from Thursdays to Sundays.
www.desertdoor.com

SHOPS
THE BEST RETAIL THERAPY AND WHAT TO BUY

Unlike the rest of Texas, Austin isn't mall-focused, and independent enterprises have always been valued here, as has artisanry and the honest pursuit of making things by hand. East Austin has the main concentration of doers and designers. Fashion labels House of St Clair (see p092) and Miranda Bennett Studio (1211 E 11th Street, T 512 432 5121), which proffers ethical ladies' clothing, reflect the city's relaxed vibe, while Helm (Suite 101, 1200 E 11th Street, T 512 609 8150) makes appropriately rugged boots and shoes. In the same creative complex as Keith Kreeger Studios (see p091), you'll find statement jewellery by Lisa Crowder (Suite 102, Building 3, Canopy, T 512 524 0364), and just down the road at another hub, Springdale General (1023 Springdale Road, T 512 416 1234), Made by Eliana (www.elianabernard.com) slipcasts beautiful marbled ceramics.

On the S Congress Avenue strip, there's menswear at 'modern-day general store' Stag (No 1423, T 512 373 7824), custom hats at Maufrais (No 1512, T 512 945 9905) and cowboy boots at Tecovas (see p034). Elsewhere, Waterloo Records (600 N Lamar Boulevard, T 512 474 2500) is an institution, and for a contemporary take on the state's leatherworking heritage, check out Noah Marion (2053 S Lamar Boulevard, T 512 981 6692) and Natalie Davis' online Canoe (www.canoegoods.com). For more mementos, pick up deli items at Salt & Time (see p094), and a bottle of the local hooch (opposite).
For full addresses, see Resources.

ARCHITOUR

Austin Central Library
Lake Flato and Shepley Bulfinch's library, opened in 2017, was the kind of civic space Austin needed. It has reading nooks, group study sections, work stations and a tech 'petting zoo' for trying out gadgets. At its heart, a dramatic six-storey atrium pulls daylight down to the lowest levels and is crisscrossed by staircases and walkways: a dynamic circulation tool. Up on the roof, a butterfly garden overlooks Lady Bird Lake.
710 W Cesar Chavez Street, T 512 974 7400

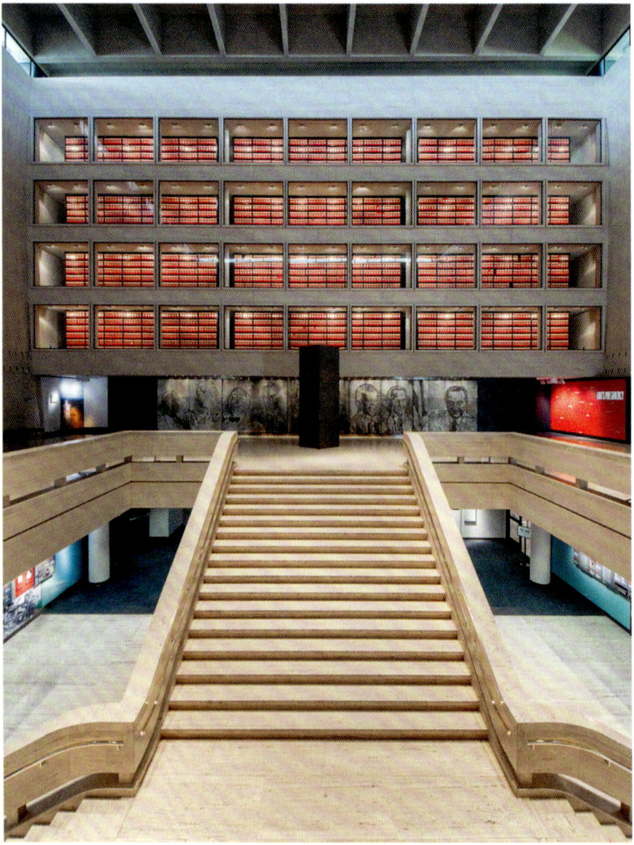

LBJ Presidential Library
Following the assassination of JFK, Lyndon B Johnson's presidency (1963-1969) marked a tumultuous period in US history, from the civil rights protests to the Vietnam War. This archive and museum was unveiled just two years after the end of his term. Its location here is in recognition of the Texan's start in politics, as a congressman representing Austin, and of his retirement to his family ranch near Stonewall, about 100km west. Gordon Bunshaft designed a structure as serene as LBJ's tenure had been turbulent, with travertine walls rising from a podium in a slight curve up to a cantilevered storey. Inside the Great Hall (opposite), four of the eight storage levels, where documents are filed in red boxes, are a captivating sight. Exhibits trace his complicated legacy and include one of Austin's oddest attractions, an animatronic LBJ that utters folksy tales. *2313 Red River Street, T 512 721 0200, www.lbjlibrary.org*

St Edward's Residential Village

The private St Edward's University has been a feature of the South Austin skyline since 1888 when its main building first towered over the area (it was reconstructed in 1903 after a fire). Galveston architect Nicholas Clayton's Victorian gothic edifice remains at the heart of the campus; in the modern era, it has been joined by designs by Sasaki Associates and local practice Andersson/Wise. Chilean maestro Alejandro Aravena's striking residential complex, on a low hill, arrived in 2008. To maximise natural light, living quarters are outward-looking, while common parts face onto an inner courtyard (above), which is fitted out with red glass to echo the tiled roofs nearby. The faceted brick walls, which vary in texture, are a nod to the limestone outcrops of Central Texas.
3001 S Congress Avenue,
www.stedwards.edu

Circuit of the Americas

F1 is not widely popular in the US yet, but if this colourful venue is any indication, the sport is on its way up. The privately funded $400m complex opened in 2012, its 5.5km track (the only FIA-certified Grade I circuit in the country) designed by German expert Hermann Tilke. Local architects Miró Rivera conceived the surrounding facilities, which include an 11-hectare plaza with a reflecting pool, an event lawn and amphitheatre, and a 9,000-seat main grandstand. The firm also devised the course's signature feature, a 77m tower with a veil of bright-red steel tubes that are intended to echo tail lights. If you can't make a race or catch a concert in the arena, book a tour of the track and VIP areas. Or, for a hands-on experience, splurge on a half- or full-day racing lesson. *9201 Circuit of the Americas Boulevard, T 512 301 6600, www.circuitoftheamericas.com*

081

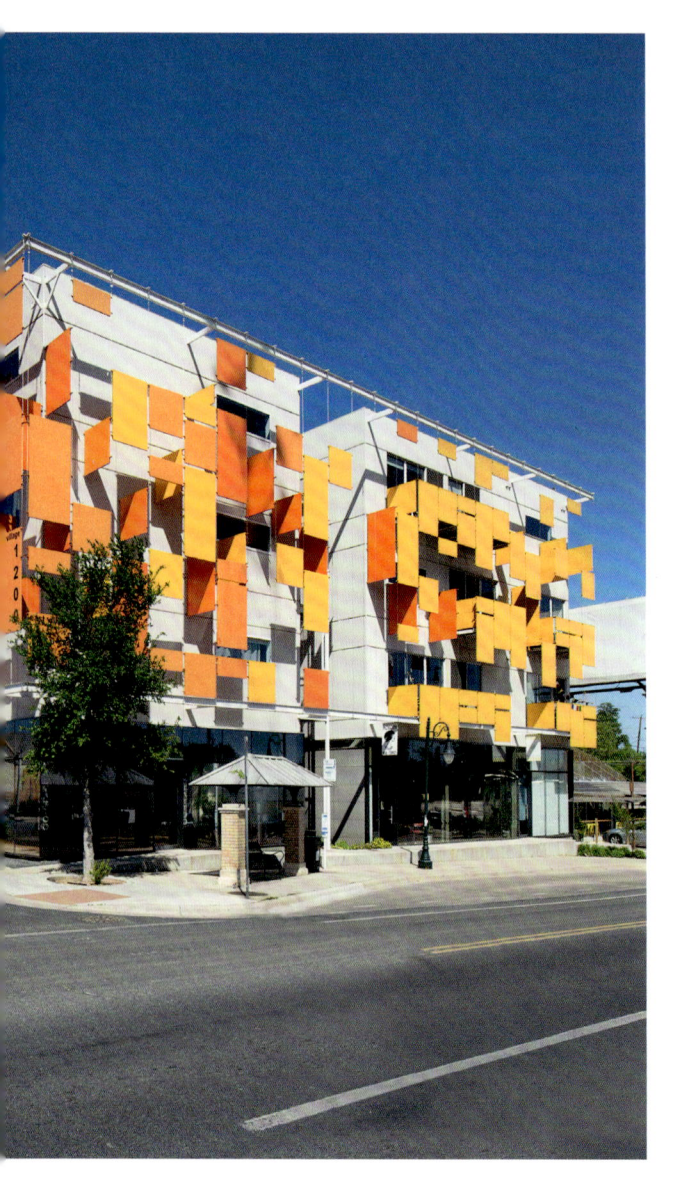

ARCHITOUR

The East Village

To borrow a Texan saying: you can't swing a dead cat in East Austin without hitting an example of gentrification. In many cases, this has consisted merely of sprucing up existing storefronts and bungalows, but there is plenty of new construction too. If only it were all as alluring as this 2010 mixed-use complex by Austin firm Bercy Chen Studio. Above the glazed retail units at street level there are three storeys of apartments faced in white metal. Brightly coloured steel panels seem to free-float around the building, making an aesthetic statement while fulfilling the functional roles of balcony railings and solar screens. In order to deliver a sustainable structure, the architects used energy-efficient glass and recycled materials, and native plants for the landscaping and a green roof.
1200 E 11th Street

City Hall

In collaboration with Cotera, Kolar, Negrete & Reed, New Mexico firm Antoine Predock created an idiosyncratic local government HQ on a conspicuous lakefront site bang in the centre of Austin. Inaugurated in 2004, the low-slung structure plays off both the natural and built landscapes. Its skewed floor plates are a counterpoint to the rigid Downtown street grid, and the limestone and copper skin references the Balcones Escarpment – the ridge that defines the surrounding topography. A limestone wall that rises from the subterranean car park through the four-storey atrium drives the idea home, literally anchoring City Hall to the bedrock. Crowning it is a folded copper roof, part of which protrudes out over 2nd Street in a 15m taper dubbed the 'stinger'.
301 W 2nd Street, T 512 974 2000,
www.austintexas.gov

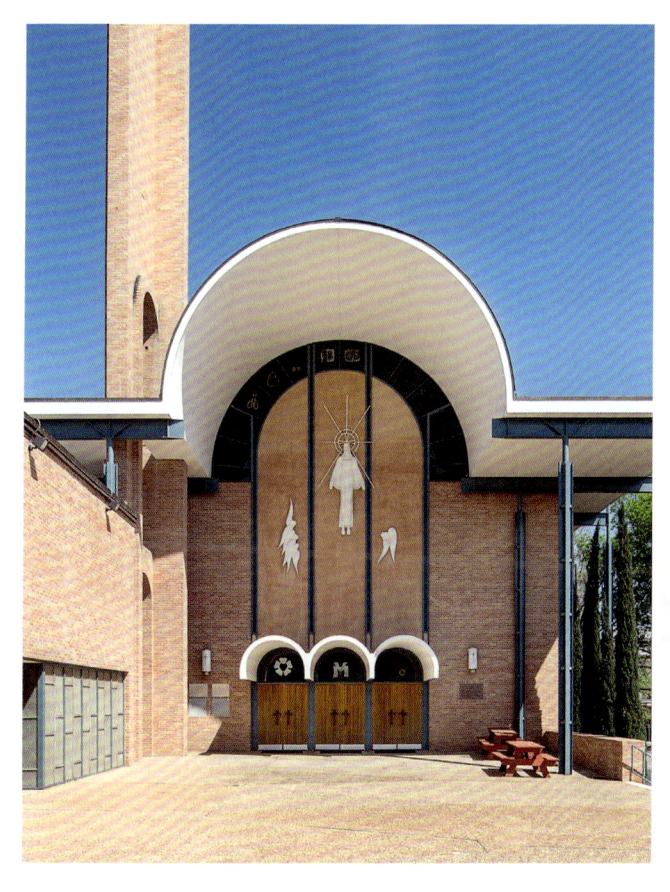

St Martin's Ev Lutheran Church

This modernist church is unique in Austin. Constructed in 1960, it was conceived by local architects Jessen Jessen Millhouse & Greeven. Lead designer Robert George Mather studied under Mies van der Rohe and worked with Walter Gropius, and the influence of both is clearly discernible in this interpretation of a Roman basilica. Taut, planar walls have been rendered in pink brick and slender steel columns form the exposed structural system supporting an amazingly thin concrete barrel vault. Other elements impress too: the sculptural triptych above the entrance is by Charles Umlauf (see p064), an art professor at UT for 40 years, and the abstract stained-glass windows were executed by Botz-Miesen in Cologne. The altar was transferred from St Martin's 1929 neo-Gothic former home.
606 W 15th Street, T 512 476 6757

ARCHITOUR

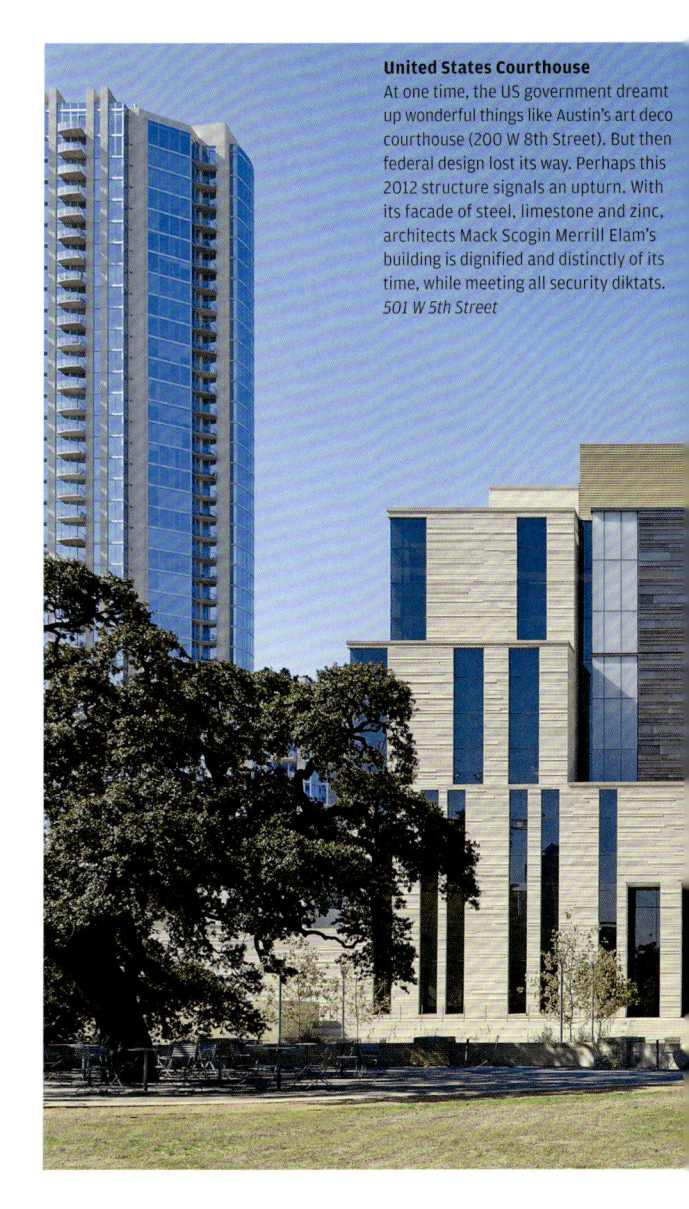

United States Courthouse
At one time, the US government dreamt up wonderful things like Austin's art deco courthouse (200 W 8th Street). But then federal design lost its way. Perhaps this 2012 structure signals an upturn. With its facade of steel, limestone and zinc, architects Mack Scogin Merrill Elam's building is dignified and distinctly of its time, while meeting all security diktats.
501 W 5th Street

Austin by Ellsworth Kelly

Artist Ellsworth Kelly's minimalist structure at UT's Blanton Museum of Art is the only building he designed. He first planned the project in the 1980s, intended to stand in a vineyard in California, but it languished for lack of funding until the university and private donors raised the $23m to place it in Austin. It proved to be his last work: he died during the design phase in 2015, and San Antonio architects Overland Partners finished it in 2018. Kelly's fascination with Romanesque and Gothic churches shows up in the cruciform plan and soaring barrel vaults, although as an atheist he avoided overt religious symbolism. Instead, it is a temple to colour, shape and form, with the kaleidoscopic arrangements of tinted glass bathing the interior in ever-changing light.
200 E Martin Luther King Jr Boulevard, T 512 471 7324, www.kellyattheblanton.org

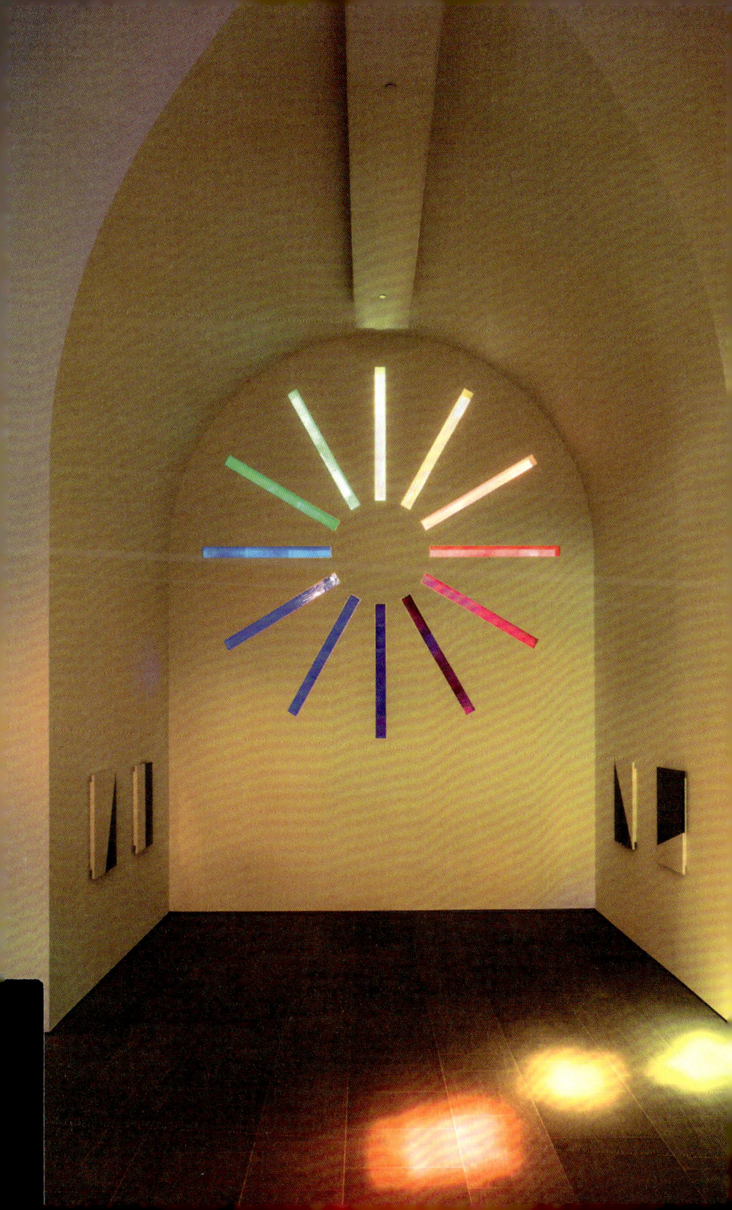

One Eleven Congress

Formerly Austin's tallest building, this 30-storey office tower is not the high point it was in 1987 but remains prominent thanks to its lakefront site and stepped geometric profile, which was partly dictated by a 1931 law aimed at protecting panoramas of the Capitol dome. Architects Victor Lundy and HKS designed it as a parallelogram that slices diagonally through its plot, sheathed in bronze glass and the same 'sunset red' granite used on the statehouse. The skewed footprint allowed room for a sunken plaza that now serves as seating for Fareground food hall (see p048), which MHOA carved out of the lower lobby in 2018, replacing the marble and brass with geometric tiles and hardwood floors and delicate screens that interact beautifully with the original patterned Burmese teak ceiling.
111 Congress Avenue

ARCHITOUR
A GUIDE TO AUSTIN'S ICONIC BUILDINGS

Settled from the 1830s, Austin began as a tiny frontier town. Some remnants of that era survive, like the 1854 Governor's Mansion (1010 Colorado Street, T 512 305 8524), but development only truly began when the railway arrived in 1871, sparking a boom that resulted in the Victorian buildings that still dot the centre, notably the opulent 1886 Driskill Hotel (604 Brazos Street), financed by a cattle baron.

The 20th century brought larger, more sophisticated structures. The 1910 Scarbrough Building (101 W 6th Street) was the city's first skyscraper, the 1929 neo-Gothic Norwood Tower (114 W 7th Street) was another early stab at the heavens, and the 1938 Herbert Bohn House (1301 W 29th Street) is the state's best example of art moderne. But it wasn't until the 1960s that local architecture started to attract wider attention, thanks to projects such as St Martin's Ev Lutheran Church (see p078) and SOM's LBJ Presidential Library (see p084).

These days, the skyline is in constant flux but many of the most daring schemes do not shout from the rooftops – Antoine Predock's City Hall (see p079) drew praise for fusing contemporary forms with materials that reflect the terrain. Other accomplished under-the-radar builds include St Edward's Residential Village (see p083), Alterstudio's Texas Hillel: The Topfer Center for Jewish Life (2105 San Antonio Street) and, should you require a stylish comfort break, Miró Rivera's outdoor trail restroom (see p031) at Lady Bird Lake. *For full addresses, see Resources.*

Big Medium

Shea Little, Jana Swec and Joseph Phillips formed Big Medium in 2007 to draw on the success of their East Austin Studio Tour and the Texas Biennial, a state-wide open-call exhibition. They were also the driving force behind Canopy, a trio of industrial buildings reimagined by MHOA as studios, galleries and shops, and moved into a high-ceilinged space here in 2013. The gallery champions emerging talent like local sonic guru Steve Parker, Austrian multimedia star Cordula Ditz and LA painter Augustus Thompson. Group shows often tackle themes, such as nature, in 'Unity of Opposites' (above), by Mexican street artist Blasto and sculptor Ernesto Walker, and belonging, in 'No Me Olvides', which featured eight Austin-based Latinos. Tuesday to Saturday, 12pm to 6pm.
101 Building 2, 916 Springdale Road, T 512 939 6665, www.bigmedium.org

Lora Reynolds Gallery

For a city that trumpets its creative scene, it has few top-tier galleries of this calibre. Lora Reynolds worked with Matthew Marks in New York and Anthony d'Offay in London before going solo in 2005, and exhibitions here are consistently sophisticated. She mounted the first US show of Tom Molloy's drawings, premiered Turner Prize nominee Phil Collins' 'El Mundo No Escuchará/The World Won't Listen' and represents major artists including Austin natives The Haas Brothers, Brooklyn painter Jim Torok and Japanese paper-sculptor Noriko Ambe. In 'Federal Triangle' (above), Mike Osborne investigated paranoia and surveillance in the political heart of Washington DC via eerie black-and-white photography. Open Wednesday to Saturday, 11am to 6pm.
Suite 50, 360 Nueces Street,
T 512 215 4965, www.lorareynolds.com

ART/DESIGN

Mass Gallery

A collective of artists, musicians, writers and educators established in 2006, Mass has transplanted operations around town, including a spell organising pop-ups and public art projects, before settling in this old ceramics studio on the east side. For its 2018 inauguration, group show 'Staycation: Thresholds' (above), the third iteration of a series championing Austin talent, featured work by 10 locals including Sunday Ballew, Levi Dugat, Emily Cross and Andrew Hulett, who ricocheted sound around the gallery from suspended tubes and panes. Next up came 'Interwoven', which highlighted city embroiderers Fort Lonesome and Navajo weaver Melissa Cody. There are regular tie-in performances and screenings held on the adjacent lawn. Open Friday to Sunday.
705 Gunter Street, T 512 535 4946, www.massgallery.org

Brandon Mike

Multidisciplinary designer/artist Brandon Mike believes that every object possesses beauty, and his minimal nature-inspired pieces certainly do. His preferred medium is concrete, which he moulds into swirling sconces ('Sun Spiral'), sleek bowls ('Lunah') and stylised animal figurines such as 'Evo the Elephant'. These decorative hand-cast wax-polished statuettes come in a variety of colours and finishes, and can be infused with brass or given a coat of bronze. Mike's exploration of form is on full display in the elegant 'Poise' rocking chair (above). An exercise in geometry, the body is a circular band of rusted steel supporting a quartz-imbued concrete seat. At rest it is in perfect balance, as sculptural as it is practical. Visit his studio by appointment online or find his work at By George (T 512 441 8600).
www.brandonmike.com

Grayduck Gallery

Minnesotan Jill Schroeder is on a mission to make the arts accessible, and launched Grayduck in south Austin in 2010, relocating to a converted century-old bungalow in the newly happening east side four years later. It hosts up to eight exhibitions a year that mostly champion Texan artists – in 'When They Appear' (above), San Antonian Larry Graeber and Dallas-based Marilyn Jolly explored the human relationship to time and space through sculpture, painting and mixed-media collage. There are also poetry readings, screenings, gigs and events like a shadow puppet show that accompanied Sarah Fox's depictions of fantasy animals. Original elements of the property, notably an inviting front porch, contribute to the relaxed feel. Open Thursday to Sunday.
2213 E Cesar Chavez Street, T 512 826 5334, www.grayduckgallery.com

Mystic Raven

David Deming taught at UT for more than a quarter of a century and was the dean of the College of Fine Arts from 1996 to 1998. His welded-steel *Mystic Raven* was installed in a plaza on Congress Avenue in 1983. Its abstract form variously evokes a machine, a human figure and 'the spirit of a bird' and balances on an irregular tripod that lends it a dynamism evoking migration to Austin in the 1980s and the development of the city. It was restored by The Contemporary (see p028) and placed here in 2017 as part of the community project Museum without Walls. Close by, the UT campus' superb art collection includes Sol LeWitt's sculpture *Circle with Towers*, José Parlá's epic mural *Amistad América* and James Turrell's *The Color Inside*, best seen at sunrise or sunset. *Pease Park, Lamar Boulevard/W 29th Street, www.peasepark.org*

ART AND DESIGN
GALLERIES, STUDIOS AND PUBLIC SPACES

For all Austin's recent growth and wealth, true cultural depth has yet to materialise. Not to say there is no artistic tradition: see the Elisabet Ney Museum (304 E 44th Street, T 512 974 1625), the home of the pioneering German sculptor who moved here in 1882, and the Umlauf Sculpture Garden & Museum (605 Azie Morton Road, T 512 445 5582). It displays Charles Umlauf's oeuvre in the house where he lived from 1944 to 1985, and rotating exhibitions by peers such as Fort Worthian Charles T Williams. The city also has a rich history of Mexican art, which continues at ESB-MACC (see p030).

Today, creative ventures cluster in the east, although the excellent tours of under-the-radar spaces and studios run by Big Medium (see p071) in November and May now cover the west too. At other times, the Canopy hub (916 Springdale Road, T 512 939 6665) provides an introduction – check out the shows by collective ICOSA (Suite 102, Building 2, T 512 920 2062) – as do Grayduck (see p066), Mass (see p068) and Northern-Southern (1900b E 12th Street), which has a graphic bent. In the centre, major players Lora Reynolds (see p070) and Wally Workman (1202 W 6th Street, T 512 472 7428) deal in the high end, including local painters Jessica Halonen and Ian Shults.

The design field is nascent, but furniture atelier Petrified Design (www.petrifieddesign.com) is redefining the 'Texas modern' look, and Brandon Mike (see p067) is spearheading the next generation.
For full addresses, see Resources.

063

URBAN LIFE

INSIDER'S GUIDE
TY HANEY, ENTREPRENEUR

Coloradan Ty Haney moved here in 2017 to establish a HQ for her athletic apparel brand <u>Outdoor Voices</u> (606 Blanco Street, T 512 356 9136). She calls her adopted hometown 'an oasis', both for its river setting and diversity of experiences – from alfresco pursuits such as a dip in Barton Springs Pool (2131 William Barton Drive, T 512 974 6300) to late-night karaoke at <u>Emo's</u> (2015 E Riverside Drive, T 888 512 7469), Haney says: 'There is a lot of dynamism.'

A keen shopper, she's a fan of slick emporium <u>Kick Pleat</u> (624 N Lamar Boulevard, T 512 445 4500) and vintage boutique <u>Feathers</u> (1700b S Congress Avenue, T 512 912 9779): 'On every visit I find a treasure I can't leave without.' For lunch, she likes to order snapper carpaccio at <u>June's All Day</u> (1722 S Congress Avenue, T 512 416 1722) or 'dirty Tex-Mex' at city institution Maudie's (2608 W 7th Street, T 512 473 3740), where she recommends the Grandma's Special.

When dusk falls, Haney prefers characterful spots including Dry Creek Cafe (4812 Mount Bonnell Road, T 512 453 9244), 'a fine sunset vantage point', or local dive Deep Eddy Cabaret (2315 Lake Austin Boulevard, T 512 472 0961). For a 'rowdy meal out with friends' at weekends, she heads to Justine's (4710 E 5th Street, T 512 385 2900). Nights might also end with a gig at <u>Antone's</u> (305 E 5th Street, T 512 814 0361) or <u>The Continental Club</u> (1315 S Congress Avenue, T 512 441 2444), both of which she loves for their 'authentic' Austin vibe. *For full addresses, see Resources.*

Lamberts Downtown Barbecue

'Fancy barbecue?' Lamberts asks, and it's a pertinent query at this modish restaurant. Both the decor and the menu are far more refined than you get at a typical BBQ joint (purists would scoff at caramelised onion jam in a brisket sandwich, and the idea of smoked trout with avocado quinoa might induce convulsions). Yet Lamberts works, very well. Laurie Smith's interiors subtly enhance the landmark 1873 building with modern lighting and pea-green banquettes. The food also has contemporary leanings: brisket rubbed with coffee and brown sugar and smoked quail stuffed with Mexican rice accompanied by a cheese enchilada. Small plates are available at the bar; we ordered the crispy wild boar ribs piled with honey, sambal and Cabrales, and a Prickly Mule.
401 W 2nd Street, T 512 494 1500, www.lambertsaustin.com

Barley Swine

Bryce Gilmore's locavore eaterie has been rammed since 2010, for very good reason. His brilliantly executed seasonal cuisine, expressed in dishes like blackened redfish with smoked plum and couscous, features ingredients sourced from local farms and ranches, and the rear garden. Past tasting menus have listed shishito pepper tamale; Muscovy duck served with avocado and green tomato chilaquiles; and sweetcorn mochi in caramel sauce. Beers are mainly Texan and cocktails are quite playful: the signature Can I Chick It? (Yes You Can) is made with fried chicken-washed tequila, allspice butter, blueberries, ale and lemon and comes with crispy chicken skin. Levy's interior strikes a rustic note through wood beams and exposed brick. Dinner only.
*Suite 400, 6555 Burnet Road,
T 512 394 8150, www.barleyswine.com*

URBAN LIFE

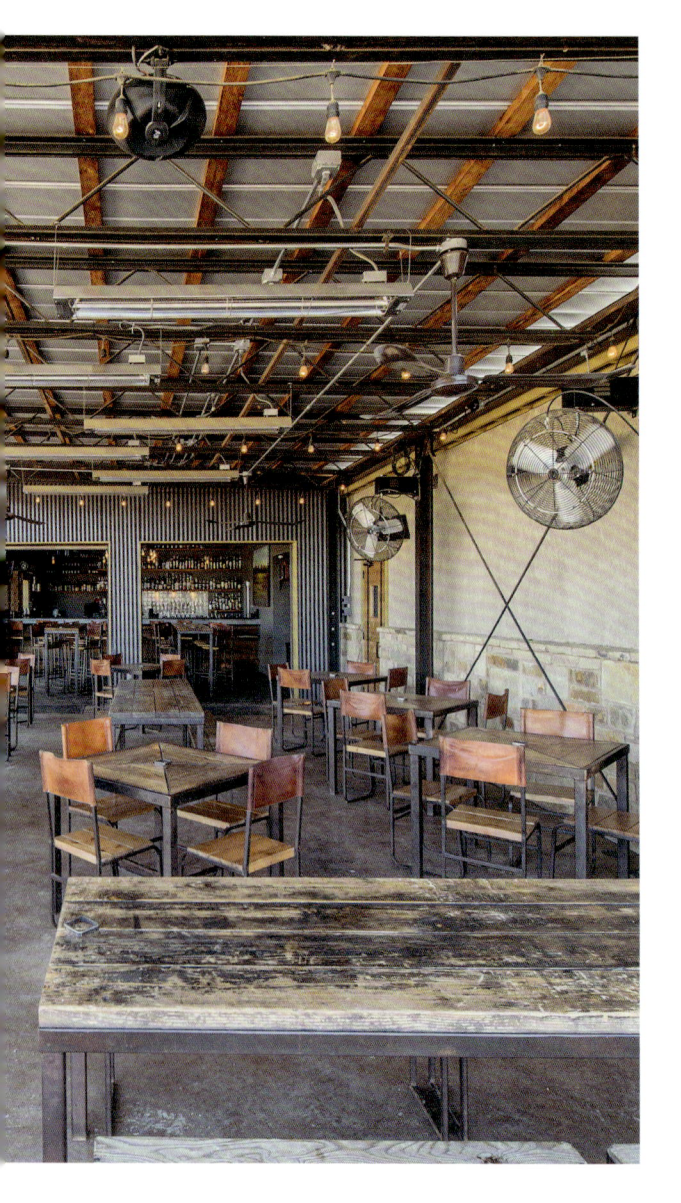

Contigo

The team behind Contigo Ranch in south Texas (see p097) opened this restaurant in 2011 to import some rural ambience into the city. The experience is mostly outside, with tables on a covered patio (enclosed by glass garage doors when necessary) and spread through the yard; inside, a former welding shop, there are 20 seats around the bar. Highlights on the seasonal menu have included tacos made with fish fried in beef fat and sprinkled with tobiko, flat iron steak with cheddar grits, and roast sweet potato with jalapeño, pickled red onion, cashews and barley. Or come for Sunday brunch – the eggs Benedict with whipped feta and pickled green tomato won us over. The well-conceived cocktails are another draw: the Desert Night mixes mezcal, plum and mesquite, and the Vesper Lynd blends pisco, bergamot and grains of paradise.
2027 Anchor Lane, T 512 614 2260, www.contigotexas.com/restaurant

Loro

Celebrated restaurateurs Tyson Cole and Aaron Franklin teamed up to launch Asian smokehouse Loro in 2018. The result is as good as expected, even for non-carnivores. True, meat is the attraction, from the prime bavette topped with shishito salsa verde to brisket with chilli gastrique and Thai herbs. But vegetarian dishes shine too, notably sweetcorn fritters with sriracha dip, and garlic rice noodles with currants, cashews and pineapple. Craig Stanghetta and MHOA conceived the place as a Japanese-tinged Texas dancehall. That translates as plenty of wood, including shou sugi ban walls, and communal tables beneath a skylit peaked roof. It's no reservations so expect a queue at dinner; arrive before 7pm, or wait with a frozen mango sake slush at the outside bar.
2115 S Lamar Boulevard, T 512 916 4858, www.loroaustin.com

Mattie's

Austinites of a certain age have a soft spot for Green Pastures, a fine-dining mainstay since 1946. New owners took over in 2015 and, after a thorough overhaul of the 1895 farmhouse, renamed the restaurant after former longtime resident Martha 'Mattie' Miner Faulk. The southern cooking is spot on for the setting. Follow a starter of fried green tomatoes or buttermilk biscuits and local honey with classics like pork ribs or shrimp and grits. Joel Mozersky's interiors retain a homely feel, fireplaces have been refurbished, and furnishings are a brilliant Victorian and midcentury mash-up. Sunday brunch here is a city tradition, especially when it involves the legendary Milk Punch (bourbon, cognac, rum, vanilla cream and nutmeg) and a stroll around the grounds.
811 W Live Oak Street, T 512 444 1888, www.mattiesaustin.com

Bar Peached
Eric Silverstein had a big hit with food truck Peached Tortilla in 2010, and transitioned its success into brick and mortar (T 512 330 4439) five years later. Not surprisingly, his laidback Bar Peached has also been packed since launch in 2019 – and there is a lot to like. Design Hound reworked a Clarksville bungalow into a cheery venue with pops of turquoise and yellow and a portrait of Lady Bird Johnson; down below is a chilled-out shaded patio. Standouts on the southern US/Asian menu include spiced cauliflower tacos, chilli crab presented on milk bread, mapo bolognese made with chow fun, five-spice pork and whipped tofu, and *bingsu* (Korean shaved ice) desserts with flavours like caramel and sea salt. Several cocktails incorporate yuzu, lemongrass and ginger.
1315 W 6th Street, T 512 992 0666, www.barpeached.com

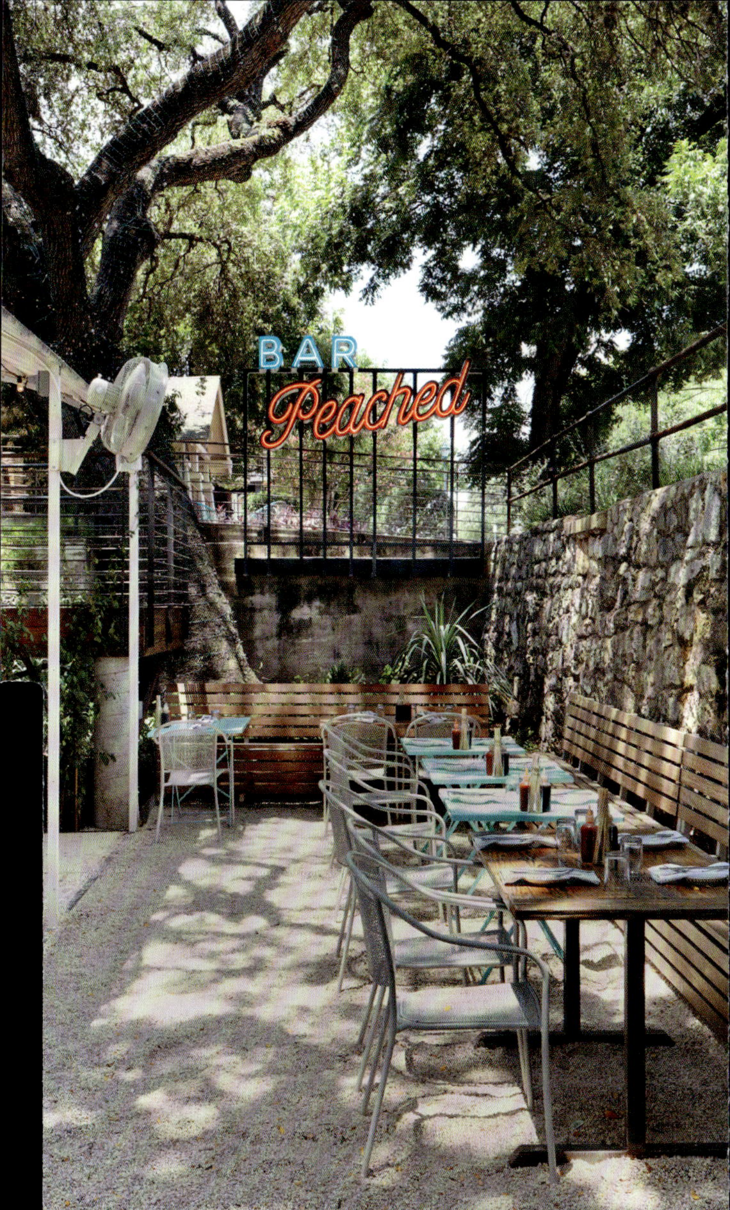
BAR
Peached

Easy Tiger

The domain of 'head dough puncher' and industry veteran David Norman, this bakery and beer garden opened in 2012. All bread and pastries, as well as smoked meats and condiments, are produced on the premises, and the menu champions locally sourced ingredients. In the morning, pick up a *pain au lait* stuffed with scrambled egg, scallion, provolone and pastrami, and a Bengal spice latte. From lunchtime, in the downstairs garden, pretzels and all manner of breads, charcuterie and homemade sausages like the bratwurst (pork, veal, sauerkraut and mustard) are served, and dozens of draught beers include Austin craft brews. Veronica Koltuniak skilfully handled Easy Tiger's dual identity, and the lower level is a melange of colonial taproom and Victorian pub.
709 E 6th Street, T 512 614 4972, www.easytigerusa.com

Eberly

There's nothing in Austin quite like Eberly, the sprawling restaurant launched in 2016 by ex-Stubb's owners Eddy Patterson and John Scott. Designed by Mickie Spencer, its nearly 1,400 sq m contain a 1960s-esque dining space complete with curved wood-panelled booths and brass lamps, a skylit 'study' inspired by the Palm House in Kew Gardens and a tiled section (above) with a 150-year-old mahogany bar salvaged from the legendary Cedar Tavern in NYC, once a haunt of expressionist painters and beat poets. From the modern US menu, try fluke crudo with sweet and spicy peppers; cornmeal hushpuppies served on lentil jambalaya; grilled squash with fava-bean tabbouleh; or tagliatelle with veal and pork ragu. Dinner and weekend brunch only.
615 S Lamar Boulevard, T 512 916 9000, www.eberlyaustin.com

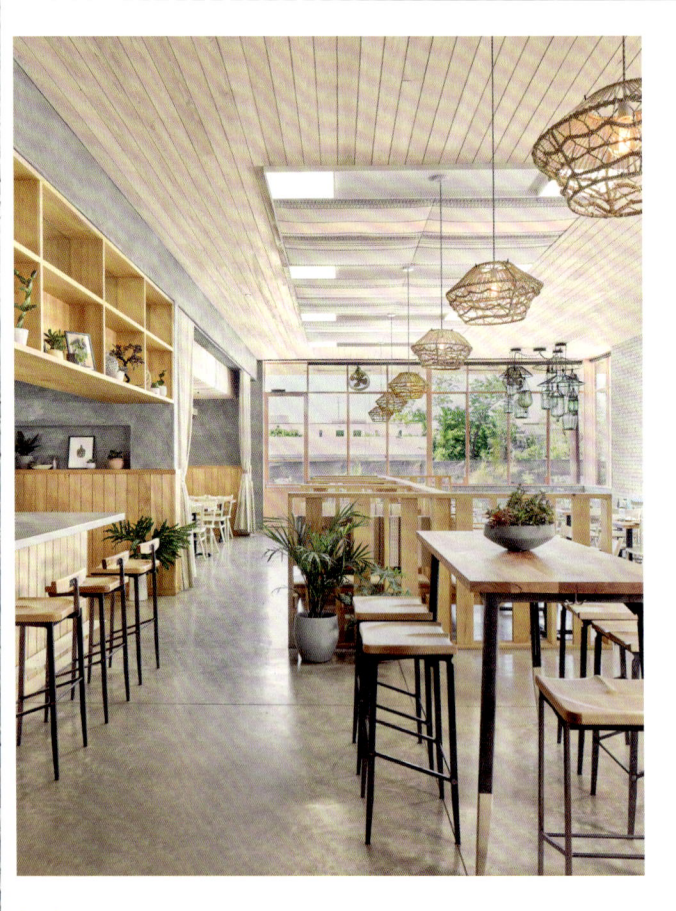

Suerte

Tex-Mex has always been a staple here, but lately there has been a boom in authentic Mexican restaurants. Suerte's speciality is masa (dough from locally sourced corn). It is handmade each day as the basis for chef Fermín Núñez's cuisine: fried tlacoyos have fillings like oyster mushroom, cabbage and jalapeño-garlic salsa, and tortillas wrap beef brisket confit (tacos) and accompany the goat barbacoa, along with mint sorrel yoghurt. At weekend brunch, lighter items include shrimp tostada and corn pudding tamal with hominy and egg. Allison Burke's interiors incorporate tabletops of pecan wood and bottles of mezcal fashioned into statement chandeliers, and the grey-and-pink upholstery and wall coverings were designed by Oaxacan Arturo Hernández.
1800 E 6th Street, T 512 953 0092,
www.suerteatx.com

Jeffrey's

When Jeffrey's was relaunched in 2013, it had already been a fixture for four decades, one of the few fine-dining destinations from the days before Austin had any real scene. It brought back the upscale yet casual feel that put the place on the map, producing a very good restaurant indeed. Mark McCain's French-US menu imbues seafood and chops with inventive, ingredient-driven flavours; try the signature fried gulf oysters served with melted leeks and cider emulsion. The real stars are the steaks, though, especially dry-aged Wagyu cuts from the south Texas town of Yoakum. Conceived by Clayton & Little with Mark Ashby Design, the elegant rooms deftly mix pattern and texture. The clubby bar is an excellent spot for a digestif and a made-to-order soufflé. Dinner only.
1204 W Lynn Street, T 512 477 5584, www.jeffreysofaustin.com

URBAN LIFE

Ellis

This slick cocktail bar was launched in 2019 to act as a shop window for the food hall at the base of One Eleven Congress (see p073). On offer are dishes from all of Fareground's vendors, including an outpost of Contigo (see p058); Israeli street stall Tlv; and Dai Due, a taqueria that specialises in Gulf of Mexico-caught fish and Texas Hill Country (see p097) wild boar. MHOA designed the freestanding building as a wedge pointing towards the street; there's seating around a limestone-backed bar in a glass-walled interior, and a few outdoor stools, but our favourite perch is the rear loggia, which overlooks a lawn picnic area. The drinks list features eight rotating local beers and seasonal cocktails like the King Bee (gin, Italicus, Dolin Blanc and sparkling water). *Building 2, 111 Congress Avenue, www.ellisofaustin.com*

Juniper

Chef-owner Nic Yanes' menu marries the fundamentals of northern Italian cooking (he travelled the entire country to learn its cuisine before setting up Juniper in 2015) with ingredients sourced from local farms and ranches. Antipasti such as chicken liver mousse with lambrusco gelée, served with foccacia, set the stage for rich pappardelle topped with short-rib ragu; basil tortellini in tomato brodo; and mains like grilled New York strip steak with herb salad. Architect Chris Sanders and designer Mark Cravotta carved the dining room out of an old Pepsi bottling plant, countering exposed concrete and lofty ceilings with walnut, Belgian oak and blue velvet to create an ambience that is at once industrial and warm. Bag a seat at the chef's counter for a view of the action.
Suite 304, 2400 E Cesar Chavez Street, T 512 220 9421, www.juniperaustin.com

Lucy's Fried Chicken

James Holmes built a tight fan base at the now-shuttered upscale comfort-food haven Olivia and his audience grew in 2010, when the chef fried up some 4,000 birds for the huge ACL Fest music event. It was then that Holmes decided to open a chicken joint in south Austin – the kind of place that would bring to mind the city of old, he said. And hence Lucy's, named after his daughter and grandmother, was sired. His fabulous crispy yet succulent signature dish is enhanced by classic Texan sides, such as cornbread muffins, devilled eggs, collard greens and 'Texas caviar' (black-eyed peas marinated in garlic and tomato). MHOA's rustic design, featuring an entrance that is decorated in reclaimed shipping palettes and an interior inspired by a roadhouse, is pitch perfect.
2218 College Avenue, T 512 297 2423,
www.lucysfriedchicken.com

Greater Goods Coffee Roasters

True to the name of this socially conscious coffee concern, founders Khanh Trang and Trey Cobb donate a portion of sales to city charities. For its 2018 launch, MHOA turned a dingy warehouse into a bright, welcoming café/roastery, by retaining the fir framing, gabled roof and steel trusses, and inserting translucent polycarbonate panels that wash the interior in light. But it is the speciality drinks, served from a colourful, sculptural island, such as the Tiger Latte, infused with turmeric and spice, or the McGregor, a mix of dark rose tea, milk and syrup made by reducing local Treaty Oak bourbon, which really set Greater Goods apart from many of its rivals. Java enthusiasts may wish to book a course in the adjacent training lab, visible through a tent-like reading nook.
2501 E 5th Street, T 512 382 9857, www.greatergoodsroasting.com

2501

Houndstooth Coffee

Austin learned to love a quality cup of joe thanks in part to Sean Henry, who launched his venture on N Lamar Boulevard in 2010. It has since expanded across the state; this 2018 branch is arguably the best-looking. The design by Dallas firm Official centres around a quartz serving area and wooden bar below a sinuous dropped ceiling clad in alder slats. Countertops, a main table, butcher-block stools and a standing drink rail in white oak add warmth. Houndstooth grinds top-class beans from Henry's own roaster Tweed; pair a cup with a breakfast taco, pastries, or waffles at weekends. In the evening, there's wine, local beer and a cocktail list – El Burro is a blend of tequila, lime, blueberry tea syrup and ginger beer.
Suite 101, 2823 E Martin Luther King Jr Boulevard, T 512 243 8902,
www.houndstoothcoffee.com

Arlo Grey

The restaurant in the Line hotel ticks all the boxes: celeb host, glam decor and a menu of inventive seasonal combos, but there is as much substance here as style thanks to *Top Chef* winner Kristen Kish's talent. She doesn't put a foot wrong with dishes such as baby carrots and sweetcorn on smoked yoghurt with puffed barley, feta and snow pea; snapper crudo with champagne, melon and roast lemon glaze; and braised rabbit and gnocchi. Interiors by MHOA and Sean Knibb play off the mid-1960s architectural shell with a textured ceiling and a striking sculpted wooden bar area and decoration by local firm Michael Wilson Design, yet its front-row views of the lake steal the show. Head to rooftop cocktail bar P6 (T 512 473 1566) for another impressive panorama.
111 E Cesar Chavez Street, T 512 478 2991, www.thelinehotel.com

She's Not Here

This South Pacific-themed spot has brought a touch of tropical glam to the Warehouse District. Its design is meant to evoke an art deco Tahiti retreat, with a beachy palette, wicker lounge chairs, leather banquettes and sofas, wooden ceiling fans, leaf motifs and a mural by Mez Data. The lunch menu (Tuesday to Friday) comprises sashimi and sushi alongside 'Hawaiian plates', which match chicken katsu or sticky coffee pork with coconut rice and exotic fruits; dinner adds satay, tempura and clay pot options. Cocktails avoid full-on tiki – the moreish Dragonfly is a mix of Iichiko shochu, lychee liqueur, cardamom bitters and dragonfruit. The venue's name comes from the Japanese concept of *irusu* – being so content at home you pretend to be out if the doorbell rings.
440 W 2nd Street, T 512 888 1970, www.snhaustin.com

URBAN LIFE
CAFÉS, RESTAURANTS, BARS AND NIGHTCLUBS

This is an exciting time to eat out in Austin, as the culinary scene is really coming into its own. The buzz began at venues such as Wink (1014 N Lamar Boulevard, T 512 482 8868), an advocate of slow food and farm-to-table, and Tyson Cole's Japanese restaurant Uchi (801 S Lamar Boulevard, T 512 916 4808) – and both are thriving well into their second decade. More recently, Bryce Gilmore has parlayed food-truck success into the acclaimed Barley Swine (see p060), and rising stars Michael Fojtasek at Olamaie (1610 San Antonio Street, T 512 474 2796) and Fermín Núñez at Suerte (see p051) are putting a twist on Southern and Mexican cuisines respectively. A healthy blend of high and low is what makes things so enticing. Austinites are as likely to splash out on a prime steak at Jeffrey's (see p050) as they are to queue up for lunch at meat trailer LeRoy and Lewis Barbecue (121 Pickle Road) or for ramen at Kemuri Tatsu-ya (2713 E 2nd Street, T 512 893 5561), an *izakaya* with a Texan twang.

As for nightlife, much of the focus is on 6th Street and Rainey Street – but they tend to draw a beer-soaked college crowd, and the velvet-rope clubs will disappoint. Far better to duck into a lounge like Half Step (7512 Rainey Street, T 512 391 1877), Ellis (see p048) or Native Bar & Kitchen (807 E 4th Street, T 512 551 9947). And, lest you leave the state without two-stepping, don't miss the esteemed honkytonk The White Horse (500 Comal Street, T 512 553 6756). *For full addresses, see Resources.*

23.00 Garage

Cocktail lounge Garage launched in 2014, sequestered in the former valet quarters in the car park of the 1954 American National Bank Building (now McGarrah Jessee) — a fine example of midcentury architecture. Designer Mickie Spencer made the most of the intimate space by complementing the existing terrazzo and turquoise glazed brick with bespoke lighting and furniture and a circular bar that echoes the curves of the access ramps outside. Mixologists craft expert concoctions made with herbs and unexpected ingredients such as mole, typified by the Indian Paintbrush, a blend of vodka, rosemary syrup, bitters, lime and grapefruit. There's also an ace whisky list, taken as seriously as the music, played on vinyl through hand-built Harbeth speakers. *503 Colorado Street, T 512 369 3490, www.garagetx.com*

21.00 Comedor

Architect Tom Kundig made the most of a corner parking lot for this sleek restaurant, opened in 2019 by William Ball and Connor Oman of neighbouring cocktail bar Garage (opposite), and Austin chef Philip Speer. A facade of dark brick and glazed blocks gives way to a double-height black-steel dining room topped by a glass box that lets in light and acts as a beacon at night. Window walls are raised on pulleys to bring in a rear patio dotted with succulents. Speer, Gabe Erales and Alan Delgado's seasonal dishes marry Mexican flavours and local produce, such as bone-marrow tacos with quelites, smoked butter and hoja santa-pecan gremolata, or chocolate tamal with caramelised-milk ice cream and amaranth. The place feels as if you've been transported to a hip DF *colonia*. *501 Colorado Street, T 512 499 0977, www.comedortx.com*

19.30 Mohawk

Austin bills itself as the 'live music capital of the world' and it was this that inspired New Orleanian James Moody to set up Mohawk in 2006 in an 1890s building. Its mantra 'All Are Welcome' applies to the eclectic crowd as much as the wide range of styles booked here, from indie to pop, hip hop, rock, jazz and blues. Meanwhile, the bill is shared by big-name touring acts, performers on their way up and local favourites such as Black Pumas, Lou Rebecca, Combo Chimbita and Portrayal of Guilt. Two stages, one indoors and one out, host up to three shows every night, and various terraces and balconies increase the chance of nabbing a vantage point. It's a fixture in the Red River Cultural District, so christened in 2013, five blocks of gig venues in a once-seedy part of town. *912 Red River Street, T 512 666 0877, www.mohawkaustin.com*

18.00 Milk + Honey

Alissa Bayer brought a dose of west coast chic to Austin when she opened her spa in 2006, and there are now branches across Texas. At this flagship, unveiled in 2012 and designed by architects Baldridge, an airy reception faces the street, but the lounge (above) and treatment rooms are secluded in a soundproofed core, and warm wooden walls, fixtures and furniture, and charcoal-coloured upholstery, create a cocoon-like vibe; Michelle Bedrosian's artwork provides the decoration. From the extensive menu, the Signature Retreat package comprises a Swedish massage, facial and mani-pedi. There is an in-house range of plant-based products: Everything Oil is a multi-purpose nourishing/moisturising elixir made with argan, rosehip and evening primrose oil.
100a Guadalupe Street, T 512 236 1115, www.milkandhoneyspa.com

16.00 Deep Eddy Pool
In the brutal summers here, locals cool off in one of the various natural pools including Barton Springs (see p062) and the under-the-radar Sculpture Falls in Barton Creek Wilderness Park (1710 Camp Craft Road). Our pick for an in-town swim is Deep Eddy, which, as its name suggests, was originally sheltered by a boulder on the river bank. It was channelled into a concrete enclosure in 1916, and was immediately popular due to a temperature that stays between 19°C and 24°C all year, and sideshows like the Great Lorena and her Diving Horse, who would perform a tandem 10m jump. Alas, despite the $9 admission, which keeps the crowds at bay, there are no such attractions today. The art deco bathhouse, built in 1936, was restored in 2007 by Limbacher & Godfrey. *401 Deep Eddy Drive, T 512 472 8546, www.deepeddy.org*

15.00 Tecovas

Their stacked heels and pointed toes have roots in ranching, but durability, comfort and a classic look ensure cowboy boots are a Texas staple even in urban areas. They come in a mind-boggling range of models and materials; check out the thousands of pairs on display at Allen's Boots (T 512 447 1413). Nearby Tecovas, launched online in 2015, has a more streamlined collection of minimal styles from traditional high-shaft to the modern lower-rise. All are designed in Austin and handcrafted in León, Mexico, from calf, ostrich, python, caiman, alligator or lizard skin, and waterproof suede. There are leather bags and accessories too. MHOA designed the 2019 store in a mix of raw and refined textures, from steel and concrete to wood and leather, to evoke a hacienda.
1333 S Congress Avenue, T 512 675 4343, www.tecovas.com

13.30 Joann's Fine Foods

As a crucial part of Liz Lambert's reboot of the Austin Motel (see p016), she teamed up with restaurateur Larry McGuire for a spin on the US diner. It's a great spot for brunch as the all-day menu combines Tex-Mex fare with healthy California-inspired items. Fill up on breakfast tacos, *huevos rancheros*, pea guacamole, 'hippie' *migas* made with soy-based chorizo and a hearty *pozole rojo* stew with guajillo-braised pork, hominy, radish, kale and a poached egg. For dinner, there are Texan standbys like chicken-fried steak. The motel opened in 1938, and had its heyday in the 1950s, and Joann's elicits midcentury nostalgia with seafoam-green upholstery, panelled walls and bright-red countertops. At the weekends, you can buy a pass to chill in the kidney-shaped pool.
1224 S Congress Avenue, T 512 358 6054, www.joannsaustin.com

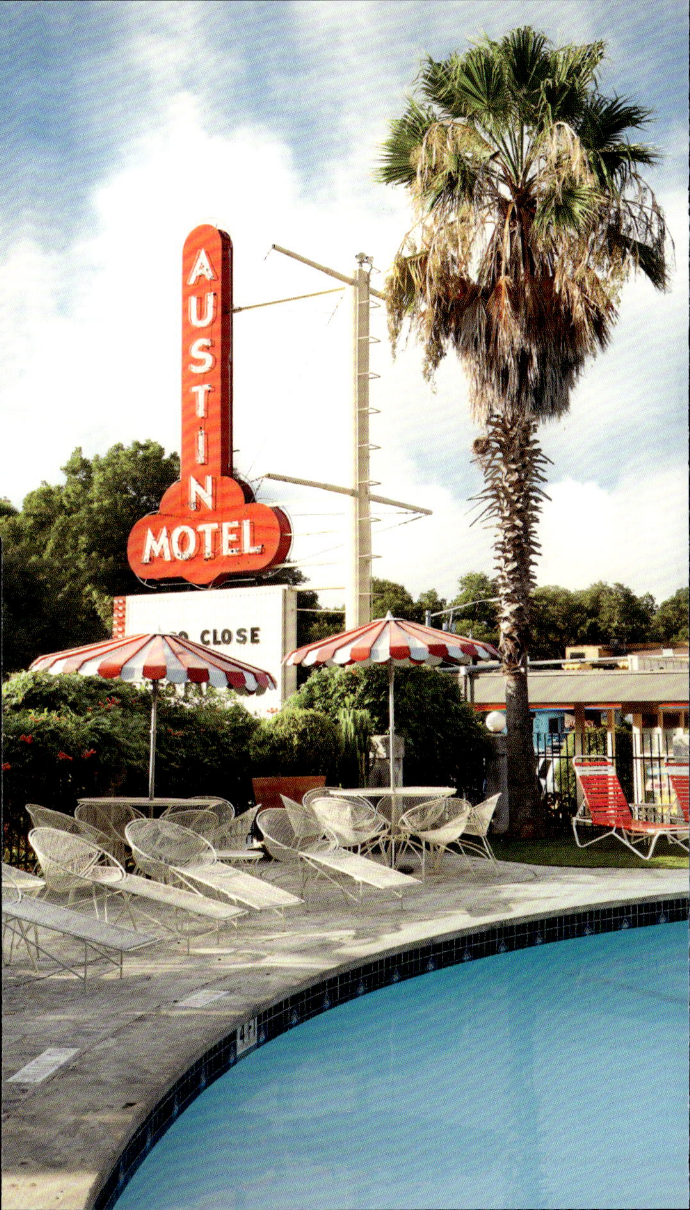
AUSTIN
MOTEL
CLOSE

13.15 Lady Bird Lake Trail Restroom

The city has invested millions of dollars in improvements to the 16km Lady Bird Lake Hike and Bike Trail over the years. Standout additions include the 2.2km boardwalk off E Riverside Drive, unveiled in 2014, which offers dazzling views as it meanders along the south shore. Less showy, but arguably more practical, is architects Miró Rivera's 2007 public loo at the end of Rainey Street. A spiral of 49 rusted Corten plates encloses a WC and shelters a rest area with a shower and drinking fountain. They vary in height and width and are staggered to admit light and air but maintain privacy. In 2016 it was joined by Heron Creek Restroom, a pair of steel and concrete tents by Mell Lawrence off W Cesar Chavez Street. These sculptural facilities demonstrate that design for even the most utilitarian places can be uplifting.
Rainey Street/Cummings Street

12.30 ESB-MACC

Proposals for a centre celebrating Austin's Mexican heritage were mooted in the 1970s but it wasn't until 2007 that the ESB-MACC arrived, due in significant part to minority rights activist Emma S Barrientos. Austin architects Casabella collaborated with Del Campo & Maru and Teodoro González de León to conceive a low-slung arc that fronts a wedge-shaped auditorium wing, faced in white concrete embedded with marble aggregate. Rotating exhibitions by Latino artists are displayed in a skylit gallery, and there are also screenings and talks. Closed Sundays. A few blocks away, the Mexic-Arte Museum (T 512 480 9373), established in 1984 by Sam Coronado, Sylvia Orozco and Pio Pulido, has a similar ethos, and puts on shows of folk art or contemporary prints. *600 River Street, T 512 974 3772, www.austintexas.gov/esbmacc*

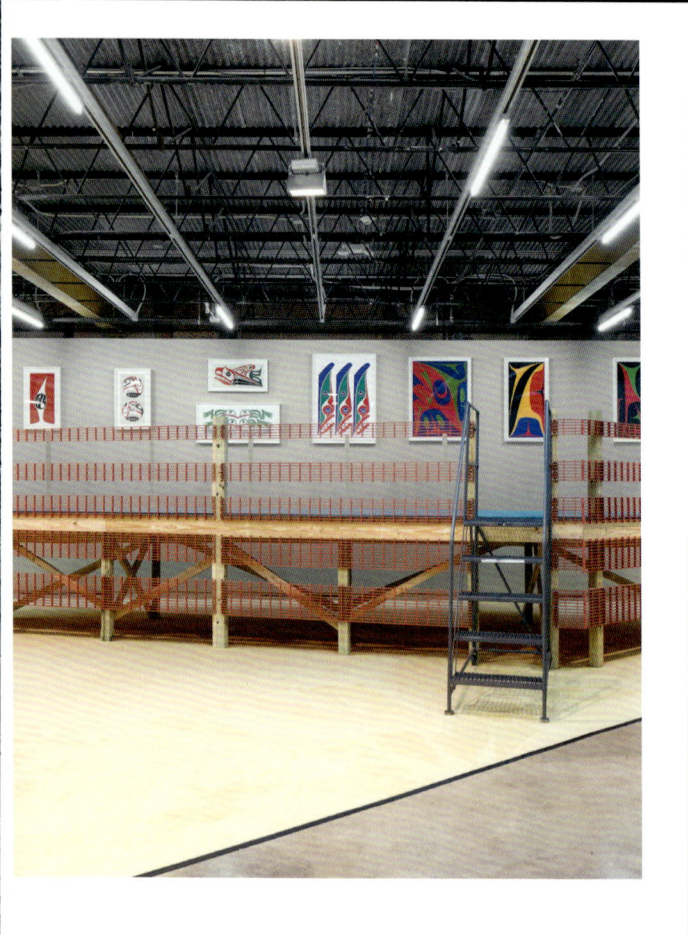

24 HOURS

11.00 The Contemporary Austin
The city's art museum is housed in a pair of very different locations: Laguna Gloria (T 512 458 8191), a 1916 villa and sculpture park situated beside the river in Tarrytown up in the north; and the Jones Center in Downtown, which is used to host rotating contemporary shows. 'Robert Davidson: U and Eye' (opposite) was curated by Jessica Stockholder, who created a framework to view pieces by the First Nations artist. The 1920s cinema was reimagined in 2010 by NYC firm LTL, who dotted the exterior with green-glass blocks and installed an ipe-wood staircase. It was expanded in 2016, when Jim Hodges' *With Liberty and Justice for All (a Work in Progress)* was fixed to the facade. Closed Mondays. In 2019, architects Trahan added two steel-and-glass pavilions and restored a gatehouse at Laguna Gloria, with landscaping by Reed Hildebrand.
700 Congress Avenue, T 512 453 5312, www.thecontemporaryaustin.org

24 HOURS

10.00 Texas Capitol
Austin's best-known landmark is the work of Detroit architect Elijah E Myers, who based his plan for the building on the US Capitol in Washington DC. The detailing is in a Renaissance revival style and the pink granite facing was quarried from nearby Marble Falls. It was inaugurated in 1888. The interiors were remodelled numerous times, slowly obscuring its history behind new walls and false ceilings. In 1983, a fire that nearly destroyed the lot kickstarted a major preservation effort. A subterranean annexe, designed by Houston practice 3D/International around an inverted rotunda (right), was unveiled in 1993; San Antonio-based firm Ford, Powell & Carson restored the original structure two years later. Start your tour in the 1857 General Land Office.
112 E 11th Street, T 512 305 8400,
www.tspb.texas.gov

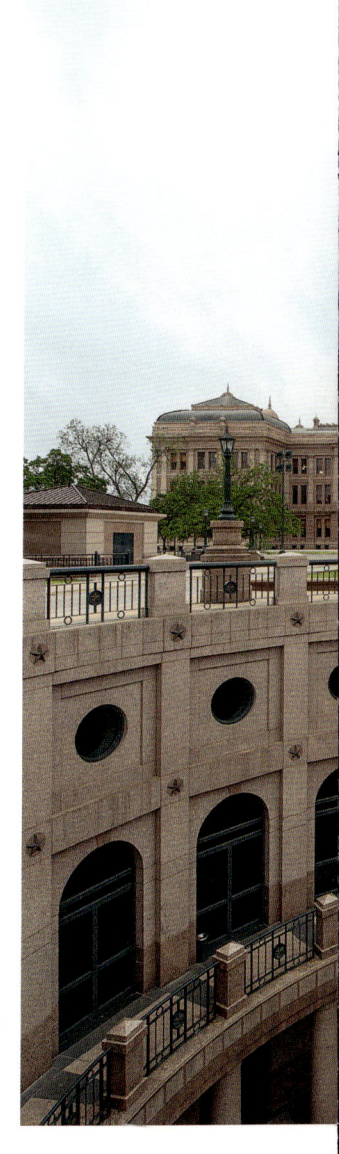

09.00 Hillside Farmacy
This characterful bistro is charming at any time of the day, but particularly so in the morning, when the sun streams in and the people-watching is best – it attracts locals of all persuasions, from hip Downtowners to pierced Eastsiders. From the 1950s to the 1970s Hillside was a drugstore, hence its new name, a play on its history and the farm-to-table provenance. The dilapidated building was restored by owners Mickie Spencer, Greg Mathews and Jade Place, who installed cabinets and display cases bought from a century-old pharmacy in nearby Elgin for the wonderful interiors. But the food is as good as the setting. For breakfast, there's eggs with ricotta salad, brioche *pain perdu* with orange maple syrup and grapefruit with brûléed sugar.
*1209 E 11th Street, T 512 628 0168,
www.hillsidefarmacy.com*

24 HOURS
SEE THE BEST OF THE CITY IN JUST ONE DAY

Many visitors come looking for Texana, and it's here in spades, from BBQ joints to honkytonks. But there is much more to Austin, from swanky restaurants to a Latino heritage and cutting-edge art. And you can't avoid music: bands play any given night in a multitude of venues. Get around on two wheels, for hire at a BCycle station.

Begin at the Capitol (see p026), from where it's an amble to The Contemporary (see p028) or ESB-MACC (see p030) for a culture fix. Nearby Lady Bird Lake (actually a dammed stretch of river) is where Austinites of all stripes exercise in the shadow of skyscrapers. Cross it for lunch at Joann's Fine Foods (see p032) and to trawl the boutiques of S Congress Avenue (see p034). Alternatively, relax in a spring-fed pool like Deep Eddy (see p035), and pad over to Pool Burger (2315 Lake Austin Boulevard, T 512 334 9747) for tiki cocktails and homemade ice cream. From March to October, don't miss a local sunset phenomenon – secure a view of Congress Avenue Bridge to witness the flypast by North America's largest urban bat population.

Start the evening by taking in a gig on Red River Street at Stubb's (No 801, T 512 480 8341) or Mohawk (see p037) before dinner; we're fans of Comedor (see p038), Arlo Grey (see p042) and Parkside (301 E 6th Street, T 512 474 9898), a champion of farm-to-table cuisine. Then explore the nightlife eastside. Kick off with a Japanese highball at quirky Domo Alley-Gato (1600 E 6th Street, T 512 893 5561). *For full addresses, see Resources.*

Kimber Modern
Secreted away in a quiet residential area, this is more stylish pied-à-terre than hotel. Kimber Cavendish and Vicki Faust found a sloping site a block removed from South Congress and commissioned Austin firm Baldridge to design it from the ground up, launching in 2008. They cleverly divided the building into discrete levels, managing to maintain a sense of seclusion from the street, although each of the seven rooms (White Suite, above) is bright and spacious, and has bespoke furniture, and artwork by locals Martha Gannon and Valerie Fowler. The courtyard, which has an oak tree as its centrepiece, and next-door lounge, decked out with Arne Jacobsen's 'Egg' chairs, act as communal zones. Margo Sawyer's colourful wall installations are a feature throughout.
110 The Circle, T 512 985 9990, www.kimbermodern.com

Hotel Saint Cecilia

Liz Lambert gave Austin's hospitality scene a jolt when she revived the 1930s San José motel (see p016) in 2000 and next looked to this 1888 estate, once occupied by one of Davy Crockett's descendants. Architects Clayton & Little turned the original house into five suites, with Victorian woodwork and high ceilings, and added nine studios and bungalows beside a heated 15m pool; a further 13 rooms and residences were incorporated in 2020. Interiors are a mix of vintage furniture and modern pieces from Droog or Jonathan Adler – in the lounge (above) are Chesterfield sofas, a 1930s art deco-style bar and a taxidermy peacock. It works very well as Saint Cecilia feels like a members' club (which it is: only guests and dues-paying locals are allowed access).
112 Academy Drive, T 512 852 2400,
www.hotelsaintcecilia.com

South Congress Hotel

When this new-build arrived in 2015, some locals worried it might spoil the small-scale character of this pedestrianised enclave. If anything, the design by Michael Hsu Office of Architecture (MHOA) actually enhances it. Ivory brick, breeze-block screens and expanses of glass lend a midcentury feel, and public lounges pull passersby into the buzzy all-day lobby. Studio Mai's interiors soften the exposed shell with terracotta and brass, and wood-and-leather furniture. All of the 83 rooms have locavore minibars, Matteo linens and films curated by Alamo Drafthouse Cinema; plump for the Milton suite (above and opposite) for its spacious patio that overlooks the rooftop pool deck. Yoshi Okai champions Texan ingredients in the slick 12-seat omakase restaurant Otoko. *1603 S Congress Avenue, T 512 920 6405, www.southcongresshotel.com*

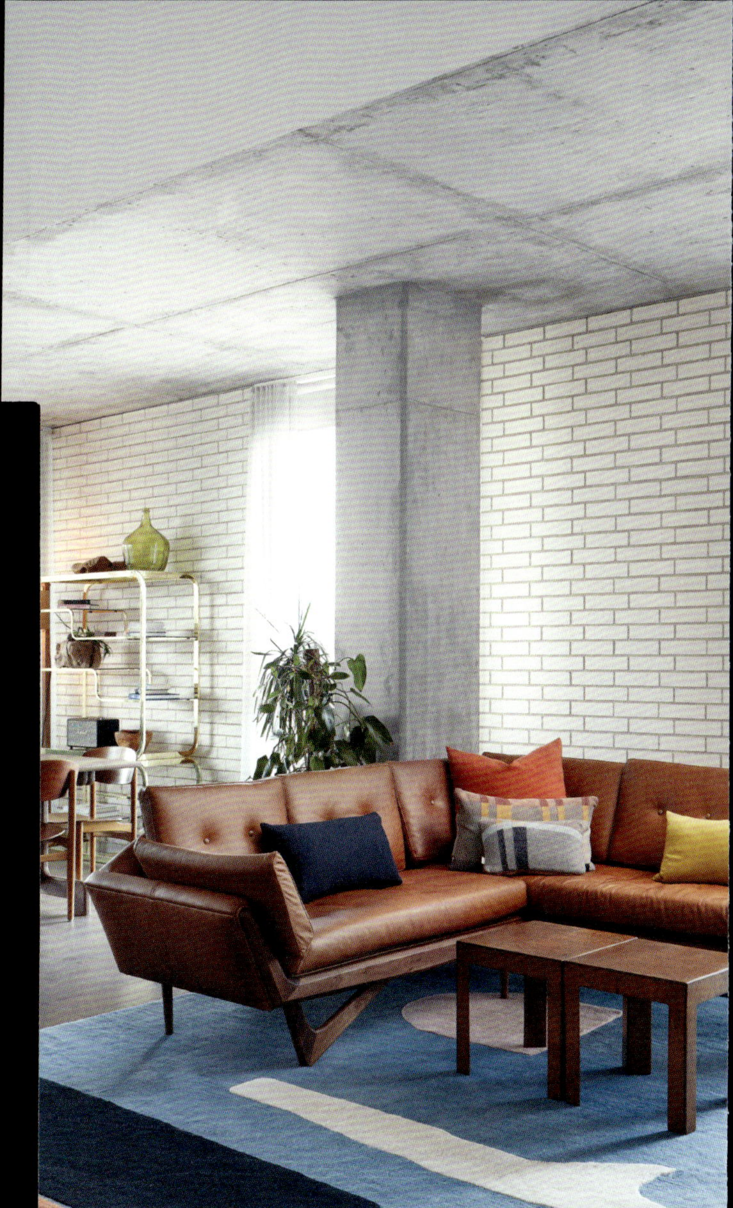

The Carpenter Hotel

Anchored by the 1949 carpenters' union hall, the draw of this boutique hotel is the local ethos. Architects Specht rehabbed the low-slung brick building to host the common areas, retaining many original elements, and added an adjacent block defined by ranks of balconies faced with terracotta to house the 93 rooms, each with a terrace. The Mighty Union devised the industrial-chic interiors. The lobby is awash with pieces by Austinites, such as side tables from Uncommon Objects, while the accommodations (Large King, above) are a riot of texture; raw surfaces are offset by bespoke furniture, like the maplewood chairs, and bathrooms clad in sapphire tiles. Chef Grae Nonas' super bistro attracts city residents with its fine Texan comfort food.
400 Josephine Street, T 512 682 5300, www.carpenterhotel.com

Heywood Hotel

Rapidly gentrifying East Austin is getting its share of cool hotels, but none are quite as enticing as the Heywood, which opened in 2012. Owners Kathy Setzer and George Reynolds hired local practice KRDB to carve out seven suites, a lobby and a courtyard on a tight lot around a bungalow that dates from 1925. Every inch has been utilised and yet it never feels cramped. The rooms, such as the King Patio (above), are done out with hardwood cabinetry and beds fabricated by Reynolds and vintage pieces. Everything combines to give the place a fashionable, laidback appeal that's spot on for the area. There's no restaurant, but it's an easy walk to great neighbourhood eateries including La Barbecue (2027 E Cesar Chavez Street) and pizzeria Bufalina (T 512 524 2523).
1609 E Cesar Chavez Street, T 512 271 5522, www.heywoodhotel.com

Kimpton Van Zandt

No hotel embraces the local obsession as readily as this 2015 opening in a new-build near Rainey Street's hip bars and cafés. The chandeliers in the lobby are fashioned from brass instruments, a music director curates custom playlists and its name is a tribute to Texan singer-songwriter Townes Van Zandt. Designer Mark Zeff has struck a masculine tone with leather and black-glazed brick in public areas, and the 319 rooms are done up in deep blue and teal. Many have lovely panoramas of Lady Bird Lake, and the spa suites have tubs set beside floor-to-ceiling windows. The theme continues at on-site restaurant Geraldine's, which proffers live performances daily and a gospel brunch on Sundays. Snag a seat near the folding glass wall overlooking the pool deck (above).
605 Davis Street, T 512 542 5300,
www.hotelvanzandt.com

HOTELS
WHERE TO STAY AND WHICH ROOMS TO BOOK

For years, Austin wasn't much of a hotel town. It didn't need to be. The bulk of its visitors were on government or university business, so there wasn't a call for stylish digs – the standout among the old breed is the opulent The Driskill (see p072). That began to change in the late 1990s, when lawyer turned hospitality guru Liz Lambert spent three years running and later revamping the down-at-heel San José (1316 S Congress Avenue, T 512 852 2350), and making a documentary about it, to widespread acclaim. She followed up in 2008 with the nearby Saint Cecilia (see p022) and then the Austin Motel (see p032) in 2017, and, together with the South Congress Hotel (see p020), they have turned the 'SoCo' area into a hotspot. Elsewhere, the refined Ella (1900 Rio Grande Street, T 512 495 1800) opened in 2014 with 47 rooms arranged around a Greek revival mansion, stylish The Carpenter (see p019) is a 2018 conversion of a union hall and, in the east, the Heywood (see p018) now has competition from industrial-chic Arrive (1813 E 6th Street, T 512 399 1927), a striking 2019 structure by architects Baldridge.

Despite this boom, there is often limited availability around city festivals and football games. Noteworthy 2020 launches, including an outpost of California mini-chain Proper (600 W 2nd Street, T 512 628 1500) and Hotel Magdalena (1101 Music Lane, T 512 442 1000), the first ground-up project from Lambert, will ease the pressure. *For full addresses and room rates, see Resources.*

Moonlight Towers

In the early years of electricity, the most efficient lighting employed a pair of carbon rods in order to create a sustained spark. These 'arc lamps' were so bright that cities across the US and Europe mounted them on tall pylons to benefit entire districts. Innovations in technology had rendered the structures obsolete by the mid-1890s, which is when Austin purchased 31 of them from Detroit. Seventeen of these so-called 'Moonlight Towers' survive today – rising 50m at the intersection of Lydia and E 11th Streets (above), for example – and are the only such set remaining in the world. Listed as both state and national landmarks, and well maintained, they are being outfitted with energy-efficient LED bulbs. They have become a treasured local fixture, and the delicate steel frames stand as a reminder of Victorian industrial skill and ingenuity.

The University of Texas Main Building

For the most part, the sprawling University of Texas campus is not especially pretty. There are high points, however, including what students like to call the 'six pack': an ensemble of tile-roofed halls set around a neat lawn, bookmarked by the Littlefield Fountain at one end and the institution's focal point (above), which dates from 1937, at the other. For its design, Philadelphia architect Paul Philippe Cret conceived a Spanish Renaissance edifice with art deco lines – a take on Texas' built heritage. The tower was originally part-used as storage space for books. It now houses offices, but the handsome library and reading rooms at its base are intact; when the university wins a sporting event, the facade is illuminated in orange. Tours (book ahead) culminate at the observation deck, which has fine views.
110 Inner Campus Drive, T 512 475 6636

Frost Bank Tower
At 157m, this was the tallest structure in Austin when it opened in 2004. It has since been surpassed but no other high-rise has trumped its style. Duda Paine conceived a two-part design: a base that references nearby heritage buildings and a silver-blue tower that rises via a series of setbacks to an exuberant art deco-style crown (critics call it a nose-hair trimmer; we say an owl).
401 Congress Avenue